THE
Berkeley
BOOK

A STORY OF HOPE, HAPPINESS, AND DOWN SYNDROME

LAURA A. SMITH

Dedication

To my incredible but otherwise private parents and siblings who allowed me to spill their emotions, thoughts, and actions onto the pages of this book so that others could be helped.

Contents

Author's Note

Dear Reader:

When speaking at retreats, ladies would often stop me in the hallway to ask if I could tell some more stories about Berkeley. Friends and co-workers always ask about him first. And not long ago, a young woman told me, "I wish I could package up Berkeley and take him everywhere with me." And so, I have written this book so that all of you can take a bit of him with you.

I have spent over 40 years loving Berkeley and doing my best to give him a safe and secure life. Because every circumstance is different, I cannot attest to the exact needs or reaction of everyone with a disability. I can only tell you what has helped our family. Therefore, the advice rendered in this book is based on personal experience and should be received with that in mind. In a few instances, I have changed the names of characters to protect their identity.

One more thought before you venture into these pages. The early events of Berkeley's life took place in 1978 – and terms that were commonly used back then can elicit painful emotions. I agonized over how to describe the days surrounding Berkeley's birth. In relating how we were told of his disability, I did use the r-word. I used it because to use any other word would not accurately depict the events and how they affected our family. This does not in any way condone the use of the word.

And now, I will introduce you to Berkeley. By the end of this book, you will join the thousands of others who already love him.

Very sincerely, Berkeley's big sister,

Laura Smith

Chapter 1
Bends in the Road

S unshine filtered through the canopy of trees over-
head drying water from the legs and bellies of our
horses. Berkeley and I gave April and Lady their
heads as they crossed the river and then struggled up
the steep embankment on the other side. I reached the
ridge slightly ahead of Berkeley and turned in the saddle.

"How are you doing, good guy?" I hollered.

"Okay," he answered with a wave and smile. Joy
emanated from his small frame, a mixture of pride and
childlike pleasure at the accomplishment of crossing the
river on his own.

The incline led us to a quiet backcountry road. Even
in the shade, the day felt unusually warm – the perfect
making for a daydream. I allowed my memories to take
me back in time to another happy period of my life.

Our family lived on a farm situated in the deserts
of Eastern Washington where the green edges of the
irrigated fields butted up to where the sage brush and
dry sandy earth took over. Grandpa and Grandma, our

nearest neighbors, lived in a house separated from ours by a space of about 50 yards. Another farmer lived half a mile down a dusty graveled road; and if we needed to reach the next closest place, we drove one of our old farm vehicles.

Berkeley came to us while we lived on that farm just after I turned eight years old, and back then I didn't understand the complexity of what the words *Down syndrome* meant or would mean for the future. The excitement of getting a baby brother far outweighed the anxiety surrounding his birth. My childhood, in beautiful innocence, continued with its simplistic delights and misfortunes.

A few months after Berkeley's birth, my grandpa gave us April, a beautiful filly; and life was good. As soon as Berkeley could walk, he would stand in the yard with his arms stretched up to me. I would grip April's sides with my legs and lean far down her left side. She patiently stood stock still as I hauled Berkeley into the saddle and settled him in front of me. With my left arm encircling his small body, we galloped up and down the long driveway.

Later, when he was older and we moved across the mountains to Western Washington, he would give me one hand and step his foot onto mine. If he jumped a little, I could pull him onto the back of the horse. For years he rode that way with his arms wrapped tightly around my waist.

When Berkeley turned 19, we bought Lady, a second horse; and now he rode by himself on our trusted April. Gradually we ventured farther and farther from home.

"Keep April on the side of the road," I shouted, coming out of my reverie. "I hear a car coming."

"Okay!" he yelled back, and I heard him gently talking to April as he guided her onto the dirt shoulder.

We had a short bit of road to navigate before we made it to the trails. But in this rural area, most people slowed down for horses. Still, I wanted to make sure Berkeley stayed safe, and I held Lady back until Berkeley caught up to me. I looked up the hill and focused on the bend in the road ahead of us. A car approached, a souped up but dilapidated automobile.

As the car drew closer, its engine alternately skipping and roaring, my horse began to prance and paw. I tightened the reins and glanced anxiously over my shoulder at Berkeley. April held steady, but I struggled to hold Lady, and then I realized the car did not intend to pass us. Engine still coughing and sputtering, it pulled to a stop alongside Berk, and guys, big teenage boys, began spilling out of it. *What were they doing? What did they want from us? Did they intend to harm my little brother?* I felt instant panic grip my insides as they approached.

Oh God, I prayed. *What am I going to do?* The beat of my heart thudded in my eardrums. *How could*

I get Berk safely away from them? Seconds ago we rode peacefully without another soul in sight, and now a gang of guys surrounded us. Everything was happening too quickly.

What are they planning to do? How did they all fit into that car? The questions in my head fired faster than I could come up with answers. *Should we jump off the horses and try to run for the river?*

No! I squeezed my eyes shut and tried to think. *That won't work. We'll never make it that far.* We had to stay on the horses, but another step and they could pull him off April's back.

"Wow, it's good to see you, Buddy," said one of the guys while he gave Berk's leg a gentle slap.

"Didn't know you rode horses," said the one shaking Berkeley's hand. Berk leaned far out of the saddle and accepted the clasps of up-stretched hands. My fear shifted, and now I worried Berkeley might fall off April as he leaned down to accept another handshake.

"Looking good, looking good." I couldn't keep track of who said what, but it didn't matter. They were his friends from school — friends I had never met.

"Hey Berkeley, is that you?" shouted the last one as he stumbled out of the back seat of the car.

The driver, who hadn't bothered to get out leaned across the now empty front seat and shouted through the window, "Keep it real, man."

And with that final word of advice, they all piled back into the car and roared out of sight.

The entire exchange had not taken more than two minutes, but I had lived through hours' worth of emotions.

Trying to still my shaking body, I wiped clammy hands on my jeans. The initial apprehension that April would spook had been replaced by sick terror and a pounding heart. When the sweet realization dawned that they were normal guys — good guys who had seen their buddy and wanted nothing more than to stop and say hello to their friend — tears of relief blinded my eyes.

That ride symbolized our life with Berkeley. Some challenges have felt like the struggle up the bank of a river. He had to work so hard at little things, and we prayed and cheered for him until he succeeded. Other times we had to stand anxiously by hoping and praying Berkeley would not fail but knowing he must conquer some difficulties on his own without interference or assistance. A few times the unknown — the bends in the road — have held us in an ugly grip of fear. But around the corner fear dissolved; and in its place came love, laughter, and knowing the world is infinitely better for having Berkeley in it.

This is the story of Berkeley – a little boy who turned into a little man and along the way impacted lives in gigantic ways.

HELP SECTION

Parents

You have embarked upon a journey full of corners you cannot see around, hills hiding your view, and what seem like endless switchbacks. But this child of yours will surprise you in so many ways. When you reach the next bend and look back, the crest of a hill and look down, or achieve that tough goal you've worked so hard to reach, you will realize that you spent more time laughing and loving than you ever anticipated possible. Take heart; your journey will be good.

Friends/Acquaintances:

Many people experience fear that they'll do or say the wrong thing when they meet someone with a disability. Remember that this person, much like you, just wants to have a circle of friends. You can join in and enjoy the journey too.

Chapter 2

The Beginning – September 1978

"I said, he's obviously retarded. Didn't you know that?" The doctor's biting words came across the telephone line calloused and cold. "Didn't you even look at his face?"

Had it only been a day ago that Mom had stood in the hallway between my brothers' bedroom and the one I shared with my sister and announced, "I'm going to have our baby tonight."

"How do you know?" I had asked.

"I just know," she replied.

"How're you going to get to the hospital?" Leigh asked.

"Ethan will drive me if Dad doesn't get home in time."

I absorbed that for half a second and imagined my brother driving Mom into town. As a 12 ½ year old farm kid, Ethan had known how to drive for some time.

Dad had been farming our grandparents land for the past few years; but at harvest time, Dad often stacked hay for other farmers. Tonight, he had gone to work on a farm several miles away and would not get home until around midnight. Even I knew babies didn't wait for dads to get home.

Grandpa and Grandma, always at home next door, had gone to an event in a neighboring town and would not be home for hours. Nobody had cell phones in those days. So, like we would do thousands of times in the coming years, we figured out together how to handle the situation.

"Ethan will have to drive me in the Jeep if Dad doesn't get home in time." Mom said it as calmly as if she were giving instructions on how to fold clothes properly — not a trace of hysteria in her voice. "So, if you kids wake up, and I'm not here, don't worry. Grandpa and Grandma will be home later; and until then, Leigh's in charge."

Leigh, slightly annoyed at not being chosen to drive Mom to town, now accepted his responsibility with a sleepy yawn. At nine years old, he could drive too even though he had to sit on the edge of the seat to reach the gas peddles. He could have driven Mom to town, but being in charge might be just as much fun.

"I'm going to go lie down now," and we listened as Mom's heavy steps took her to the other end of the house.

Amy climbed out of bed and crawled in with me. "I hope she has a boy," she whispered.

"Me too. Except I hope she has a boy and a girl. I want twins."

Amy, the baby of the family for six years could hardly wait to call herself a big sister. Whispering and giggling, we tried to stay awake and listen for Mom and Ethan to leave or for Dad to get home; but our eyes grew heavy. Without meaning to, we fell asleep.

Berkeley made his entrance into the world at 3:30 a.m. on September 13, 1978, in Soap Lake, Washington. The hospital, a small cement block building, painted white and encircled by a neat lawn, was in turn surrounded by homes badly needing paint. Broken fences enclosed the dirt packed yards. Perhaps years ago, the lawns had green grass; but now junk cars and tumbleweeds inhabited the plots. The tidy lawns of the Lutheran and Baptist churches down the street offered the eyes a small reprieve from the bleakness of the town.

Dad made it home in time, and all of us kids were still in bed when Grandma came over to make breakfast and send us off to school.

"You have a baby brother," she congratulated us from the hallway.

For half an instant I felt disappointment when she didn't add "and a baby sister," but Amy stood up in bed and cheered. The four of us ran into the kitchen and talked over the top of each other.

In the excitement of our roles as new big brothers and sisters, Grandma had to shoo us out the door,

"You're going to be late for school," she scolded. A minute later she ran after us with a forgotten lunch pail.

Always anxious to have something to tell, I planned the whole way to school what I would tell my friends. But instead of my carefully worded announcement and before my feet hit the graveled parking lot, I shouted, "We have a new baby brother."

Mid-morning our pastor picked us up from school and took us over to the hospital. "Your new baby brother is having a little trouble eating," he explained to us on the way, "He's going to be in a special crib made from glass. It's called an incubator."

As he parked the car and we walked to the hospital entrance, I tried to imagine a glass crib. I hesitated on the front steps, the concrete structure looming tall and cold before me.

"Will I get to hold him?" I asked as I fidgeted with the zipper on my jacket.

"No," Ethan answered. "Weren't you listening? He's going to be in an incubator."

Pastor opened the door and motioned us into the dim interior. Our steps echoed in the barren hallway, and even our hushed whispers made too much sound.

"Here he is," a nurse said, her voice standing out starkly against the drab walls and linoleum floor. She pointed at a picture window just a little too high for me to see through. Someone picked up Amy and held her so she could see, but I had to stand on the tips of my toes. Peering into the nursery window, I tried to make out my brother. But the darkness of his room and the glare on the window made it hard for me to see. The separation of the window and presence of the incubator gave me an isolated feeling, and I longed to get closer and to see him better. A melancholy lonesomeness filled my heart. I wanted to hold him so much and wondered why we couldn't go into his room and see him up close, but someone grabbed my hand and pulled me away.

Children were not allowed in the same room with new mothers. So, the nurse took us outside and around to the back of the hospital where Dad opened the window to Mom's room. Once again, I stood on tippy toes trying to see inside. I jumped, and as my head bobbed above the windowsill, yelled, "Hi Mom!"

"Shhh!" the nurse hushed me.

"Hi kids," Mom's answer came back bright and welcoming — perhaps a little extra cheerful to combat the grouchy nurse. "Did you see our cute baby?"

I wanted to ask Mom how long until we could hold our baby, but I still couldn't get anybody to lift me up, and I did not know how to make her hear me without being shushed by the nurse.

After about three minutes, the nurse told us, "It's not good for your mom to have her window open." And the pastor took us back to school where we wondered what was happening with our brother in the glass crib.

That first glimpse of Berkeley would have to hold me. I would not see him again for several weeks. That evening the hospital staff placed him in an ambulance and transported him nearly 60 miles to Wenatchee, Washington where doctors with better equipment could evaluate him.

At 1:00 a.m. on the 14th, not even a full day since his birth, the doctor in Wenatchee called Mom.

Waking from an exhausted sleep, she rolled over in her hospital bed and picked up the phone.

"We've discovered what's causing him to choke," he said. "The windpipe and esophagus are fused together, and there's a hole between the two."

Shaking herself awake, Mom tried to process this information. Her baby had looked so healthy, but it made sense — a hole causing him to choke while he tried to eat. She tried to think how to phrase the questions piling up in her head, but the doctor kept talking.

"This often occurs in retarded babies; so that's probably why this is happening."

Suddenly Mom was wide awake. *Was she dreaming? What was he talking about?* "What? . . . . what did you say?" Both hands grasped the telephone receiver. "I don't understand."

"I said, he's obviously retarded. Didn't you know that? Didn't you even look at his face?"

All sleepiness disappeared. "Yes, I looked at his face!" The words came out staccato and disconnected. Mom could feel her voice escalating, and when she tried to modulate it, the next words came in a raspy whisper. "He looks just like my other four children." And he had. Like a drowning woman, every minute she had with Berkeley flashed through her subconscious. *Yes, he'd been slightly smaller than the other babies, but he was alert and strong and perfectly proportioned.* She forced herself to listen as the doctor kept talking.

"He needs surgery if he's ever going to eat," the doctor continued as if reading out of a textbook. "But we'll need to wait until we confirm this Down syndrome condition. If he has it, as I believe he does, the surgery will not be necessary. We're going to transport him to Children's in Seattle for further evaluation."

In horror my mother tried to comprehend this news as once again nurses placed her baby boy into an ambulance for another lengthy ride, nearly 150 miles to Seattle.

She lay awake the rest of the night, exhausted and in turmoil. *If Berkeley had a disability, how were they planning on letting him die? He couldn't eat. Were they planning on starving him to death? Would she and Dad be able to force the doctors to perform the surgery? Would they be able to get them to do it in time to save his life?*

Some relief came at 7:30 in the morning when Dr. Hicks, a surgeon from Children's Orthopedic Hospital, called and asked for permission to perform surgery.

"Don't you have to test him for Down syndrome first?" Mom asked in confusion.

"Whether or not he has Down syndrome doesn't make any difference," replied Dr. Hicks.

When Berkeley was a mere 29 hours old, Dr. Hicks scrubbed in to perform the surgery that saved his life.

Two long weeks passed before the doctors definitively confirmed Berkeley's Down syndrome. By that time, Mom and Dad already knew in their hearts what the tests would reveal, but this was their baby, and they already loved him. Six more weeks of anxiety, trips across the mountains, and many prayers passed before Berkeley came home to live with us.

HELP SECTION

Parents

Moms and some dads all over the world have shared their personal stories with me about when they heard that the child they were expecting or had just given birth to had the diagnoses of Down syndrome or another type of disability. As I listened to or read these personal testaments, I traced a similar pattern. Initially, they felt fear closely followed by grief of varying degrees. The grief took on different forms but often centered around the child they thought they would have. The reality that the dreams they had for this child would likely not take place left a great sense of loss. Others feared that their marriage could not handle the stress or that their other children would resent this child. Later, once emotions settled, they fell intensely in love with their new babies and a new emotion followed – guilt.

"I felt so guilty for the tears I cried," said one mother. Another said, "I can't believe I wasted time grieving when this child was the best thing that ever happened for our family."

Please be kind to yourselves. Grief and fear for all of the reasons above are normal. Know that almost all couples experience some of these feelings. Often one spouse is stronger than the other and accepts the news with more ease. That's okay. You will go back and forth through life depending upon each other. Some days you will show more strength; some days your spouse will be the strong one.

Chapter 3
Our Club

"Is he going to be okay now? How much longer until he gets to come home? When do we get to see him? Did you see Dr. Hicks this time?"

Mom and Dad had arrived back from visiting Berkeley in Seattle, and we had a bunch of questions.

Dad held his hand up to stop the onslaught, and the solemn look on his face silenced us. "There's something else we need to talk about first." He held a piece of paper with a black and white picture of a little girl on the front. I could not put my finger on what or why the girl looked different to me. Mostly she looked like any other child; yet somehow, she seemed different.

I looked up at Dad, but he stared at the paper as if he wanted it to tell him what to say. If only it would give him a clue about how he should impart news to us and explain information he didn't understand himself.

"Our baby, Berkeley, has something called Down syndrome." Dad paused, but we just stared back at

17

him. "The doctors say it used to be called Mongoloid, but they don't use that word anymore."

"What does that mean?" Leigh asked.

Mom stood up and pressed her index finger hard against her upper lip.

"I'm not exactly sure what it means," Dad confessed. "I think it just means it'll be harder for him to learn things."

"Does that mean he won't be any fun?" Amy's face crumpled in disappointment.

Suddenly Dad's voice took on conviction and emotion. "It'll mean just the opposite. He'll be even more fun because he'll be a baby longer. You'll be able to hold him and play with him just like other babies."

"When's he coming home?" I asked. I wanted him home so badly.

"We don't know. Hopefully soon, but he's still pretty weak from the surgeries."

"Is he gonna be okay though? I mean, he is gonna be okay, right, Dad?" Leigh's face held concern. He had looked forward to having a younger brother too.

Suddenly I felt worried. What if he wasn't going to be okay? We all looked at Dad wanting him to tell us something to make us believe Berkeley would be alright.

"Dr. Hicks says he's a real fighter. He's getting stronger, and so many people are praying for him." Dad's words seemed comforting, but Mom had a strange look on her face, and Ethan was behaving strangely. He kicked at the gold shag carpet with the toe of his shoe, and a scowl crossed his face.

As the oldest, Ethan often acted as a third parent, and I didn't understand his sullenness. I wanted him to reassure me like Dad did. Looking at him expectantly, I waited for him to speak, but his eyes stayed focused on the floor, and his fists remained clenched in tight balls.

Dad cleared his throat and said, "You girls should pick out what he'll wear when he does get to come home."

Amy and I began to discuss whether we would dress him in the softest sleeper or the warmest.

Then Ethan spoke - his voice angry and harsh. "What are other people going to think of us? Joel will probably beat me up just for having a handicapped brother."

He didn't wait for a response. Turning away from us, I heard every intense step as he passed through the kitchen and slammed the screen door with a bang against the outside wall of our house.

We stood staring at each other in the booming silence that now engulfed us. Slowly Dad reached into his breast pocket and pulled out a couple of Polaroid pictures. "I took these at the hospital yesterday. It's a little hard for you to see much of Berk cause he's covered in tubes."

Silently, Leigh, Amy, and I crowded around Dad's hand to get a better look at our baby fighting for his life on the other side of the state. It *was* hard to see what he looked like with monitors surrounding his bed, and tubes protruding from his nose, stomach, arm, and foot. Nonetheless, I saw my baby brother, and I wanted to show him to everyone I knew.

"Can I take the pictures to school Dad, please?"

Dad paused for a long time. "They're the only pictures we have right now." His voice sounded like all the air had been pushed out of him, but I didn't pay attention.

"Please, Dad," I pled.

"If you're very careful, Honey," he finally relented.

I ran to my bedroom and got my denim book bag with the fold over top and pockets on the side. I showed Dad how I could put the pictures safely into the pocket and buckle it shut. "I'll take real good care of them Dad."

"I know you will, Sweetie," he said as he reluctantly handed them to me.

I could hardly wait to get to school the next day and start showing those pictures to my friends.

"Hey, want to see a picture of our new baby?" I asked Michelle. I laid my bag on the ground and crouched down beside it as I unbuckled the pocket. Removing the pictures, I stood and thrust the picture in front of the small crowd of kids. I was totally in my element, the center of attention.

"Gross!" Michelle said as she examined the picture. Just one word, but I felt my heart sink. Our baby was sick. He was in the hospital, but he was not gross, not even with the scars from surgery and the tubes.

Everything went out of focus as I worked hard to hold the tears from spilling out of my eyes.

The kids started to walk away, but then a voice stopped them. "Do you want to hear a story about your brother?" Miss Spurbeck the music teacher's words were directed at me, but her voice addressed the other children causing them to stop. "I heard Berkeley is strong. I heard your Dad say he's so strong that the doctors don't know what to do."

Children who had started to walk away now listened attentively. "They have to keep his arms and legs taped down so he won't pull those tubes out, but they can't find tape strong enough to keep him taped down. They're having a hard time because he keeps pulling his arms free. I guess he's a pretty tough baby."

I could see a new respect dawning on the faces of those kids, and my heart started to swell with pride. I tucked the pictures safely away in my book bag. I wouldn't show them anymore. People didn't understand. I had a story to tell instead.

That evening I took the pictures out of my bag and gave them back to Dad who placed them safely on top of his dresser before hugging me hard. He didn't ask me what the kids at school thought. I think he already knew.

Ethan kept on acting weird, but one evening a few days later he told the rest of us kids to meet him in the old red shed after dinner.

By the time we finished dinner and helped Mom clean up, it had grown cool outside. I stood in the musty shed with my other siblings. Rubbing my arms with my hands, I wished I had put on a sweater.

Ethan cleared his throat. "We're Berkeley's big brothers and sisters." He said it with determination as if this were brand new news. We nodded in agreement wondering why he wanted to talk to us without our parents. "It's our job to protect him," he continued. "If anyone ever makes fun of Berk, we're going to beat them up. Understood?"

We nodded our heads — the gravity of what Ethan said beginning to dawn on us. People might make fun of our brother. They might even try to hurt him, but families protect each other.

I felt my own hands clenching and releasing at the thought. Amy reached up and touched my arm, and in turn I bobbed my head in a silent *yes. Yes, even you, Amy, must be a guardian of our Berkeley.*

For a long minute we stood staring at each other, four children making a pact, creating a club, taking a step that would draw us together in a way most siblings are never bound.

Leigh broke the silence first. "We'll beat the living daylights out of any kids who pick on him!"

And then we all imagined ourselves slugging mean kids. The four of us would always have each other's backs, but Berkeley would get extra special protection.

With that plan in hand, Ethan found peace in having a brother with a disability. He had become the protector.

HELP SECTION – HELPING THE FAMILY

I look back on those confusing days and marvel at the wisdom God gave my parents to answer our questions. Often people reach out to the parents but don't understand that the other children in the family might be struggling with their own emotions. For Amy, she felt disappointed. She had looked forward to a new baby, and now it seemed as if this baby wasn't going to be what she expected.

I didn't comprehend what "learning slow" meant, and I really didn't care. I just wanted him to come home so I could show him off and play with him. But not everyone reacted the way I thought they should. I also grappled with the fact that I had never really seen him. The glare on the hospital window had prevented me from getting a clear look. Would I ever even see my little brother?

Leigh experienced concern. Still a little boy himself, he felt everyone's edginess. His older brother was upset, and he didn't know why. Mom had been crying, and Dad was tired. Leigh worried Berkeley would not come home from the hospital at all.

Ethan, almost a teenager reacted like a typical boy his age. He wanted to fit in with the crowd, and now something abnormal had happened to our family that would make us stick out.

Through the wise help of family and friends, we all made the adjustment and grew into a cohesive unit of protection and care for Berkeley.

Looking back on the many years of being Berkeley's big sister, I never had to "beat up" anyone. Berkeley walked into people's lives and captured their hearts on his own.

Parents

Be honest with your children and others. Do not try to hide the disability. This will only lead to confusion.

Friends/Acquaintances

If you are a friend or acquaintance of the family, look beyond the needs of the parents. Realize the other members of the family have upheaval as well. 40 years ago Donna Spurbeck told me about my strong baby brother, but I can still recall the feeling of relief in my heart when she jumped into the conversation. Those old Polaroid pictures have resided for many years now between the adhesive pages of a photo album — always a reminder to me, of yes, a baby fighting for his life, but also of a teacher who was in tune with a child's heart.

Here are some things you can do to help the siblings:

1. Congratulate the siblings on being big brothers or sisters. If not a member of the immediate family, send a card of congratulations to the children.
2. Ask the siblings how they feel.
3. Listen.
4. Do not condemn if what you hear is negative.

Childhood concerns may be as simple as wanting to know if their baby will be fun. They may take it in stride or experience fear and shock. Do not overreact but give them the support they need and perhaps some space to work through their own set of anxieties. Although they may be very young now, these "other" children will likely take on a huge caregiver role later in life. This will affect them more than you realize, and your initial handling of the situation will help them accept and love the child.

I chuckle now to think of the tenacity of us four kids, ranging from ages 6 to 12, meeting in our club like fashion to decide how we would protect our new baby; but it was an important step. We became, at that time, united in a way that most siblings never do. We didn't understand how over and over again we would adjust throughout our lives to include and protect him. We have stayed best friends with each other; and when other siblings drift apart because of distance and grown up concerns, we have Berkeley to draw us back to each other.

Chapter 4
Our Angel Had Red Hair

"Please give me another push," Amy begged.

Hopping off my own swing, I positioned myself behind Amy. Sucking in a lungful of air, I grabbed the back of her swing and pushed. Instead of letting go, I ran all the way under screaming, "Underdog" as I went.

"Higher," she shouted.

I turned around and grabbed her ankles and pulled her toward the earth. At the last second, I let go, and she and the swing flew backward and then forward high into the air. Again and again I caught her feet until I didn't dare make her go any higher. On the last pass, I took hold of her feet on the upswing and let the momentum lift me off the ground. At the top, I let go and tumbled onto the lawn.

"Hey, you slowed me down," Amy complained as she jumped off the swing and landed in the grass beside me. We lay for a minute with the grass pricking the backs of our necks.

"What do you think Dr. Hicks looks like?" Amy asked.

"I bet he's tall and strong – maybe he has brown hair."
I tried to imagine what he looked like holding our baby.
The nurses had told Mom and Dad that on more than
one occasion they had caught him holding our Berkeley
in the intensive care unit.

"It's really unusual," they told our parents, "he
doesn't have any reason to hold him; he just does."

"Do you think he's married and has his own kids?"
Amy asked.

I rolled over on my side to face Amy. "Probably not.
It takes all your time to be a doctor, and I think he's
probably lonely since he likes to hold Berkeley."

"I wish we could hold Berkeley," Amy said with a sigh.

"Me too, and I hope we get to meet Dr. Hicks when
we go visit Berky."

Hearing a car turn in at the top of our long driveway, we sat up and watched it making its way slowly
toward us. We sat staring as our pastor parked the car
and emerged from the front seat. In his right hand he
held a glass vase. Baby's breath formed a delicate halo
around a pale pink rose. As he passed us, he fumbled
with his tie, not even pausing to say "hello." Usually
smiling and joking, his face was void of emotion. He
walked in short and jerky steps as if his legs wanted to
turn and run the other way, but he forced them forward
toward the front door.

No one had ever brought flowers from a florist to our house; and it seemed odd, like he was coming to a funeral.

For a few weeks, a funeral had been our unspoken fear as we wondered if Berkeley could survive the multiple surgeries on his fragile body. Berkeley would not come home from the hospital until he turned eight weeks old; yet life, as it always does, continued plodding along right in front of us. As my parents plunged unexpectedly into this phase of their lives, Dad continued to harvest crops, Mom made meals and washed laundry, and we children left for school each day. And on this day, the pastor came to make his obligatory visit.

I wondered if Mom would be able to get the front door open. We did not use the front door. I considered telling pastor to use the back door like usual when Mom managed to force it open. In the brief passage of time while he stood on our front step, I saw something flicker across his face; and in anguish I realized he had pity written in his features. Instead of a bouquet of happy flowers, he chose to bring one appropriate for people who grieved.

As his back disappeared into the house, I shoved clenched hands deep into my pockets and whispered fiercely, "We love him. I don't care what you think. We love him."

His stay only lasted a few minutes; and when Mom let him out the front door, Amy and I went and stood beside her. Together we listened to the crunch of his wheels on the gravel driveway and watched as his car became a dot and then disappeared against the vivid blue sky. When we could no longer distinguish the vehicle from the distant puffy clouds, a heavy sigh escaped Mom's lips leaving me to wonder what she thought.

Mom turned back to the house, and Amy and I wordlessly climbed back onto our swings. I traced in the dirt with my toe and felt the day had suddenly become flat and empty.

"I just wish Berky could come home," Amy whispered.

I had felt that way too. If Berkeley could just come home, everything would be okay; but why had our Pastor looked so somber.

On the following Saturday afternoon, Mom had another visitor. This lady did not know about the back door either. After parking her car alongside of the swing set, she walked to the front door with a light step. She smiled at us and said, "I just want to have a little chat with your mom."

I recognized her from church. She and her husband had started attending a few weeks before Berkeley was born.

Fascinated, I gazed at her. On Sunday she had sat directly behind me, and I had turned to quickly peek at her while she sang. Her mouth had formed a perfect O as beautiful soprano notes escaped her throat, but what most mesmerized me was her red hair. Dad had been a redhead when he was young, or so he told us, but it had long since turned a ruddy brown.

Somehow, between getting ready for our baby and then the relentless trips back and forth to the hospital after Berkeley's birth, nobody had taken time to find out much about this new couple. Now she stood on our step knocking on the front door which always stuck shut and wouldn't open without a hard shove. Struck with sudden shyness, I could not find the words to tell her to use the back door.

At first Mom thought the knock was my brothers goofing off; but when it sounded again, three short raps all close together, she dried her hands on a towel and hurried to see who stood on the porch.

When Mom opened the front door for the second time in just over a week, the red-haired lady stood smiling on the front step. Her purse dangled from the crook of her elbow, and the other arm stretched outward to Mom in a questioning gesture. "May I come in?" she asked.

Curious about why she had come, I wanted to stay and listen, but Mom motioned for me to stay outside. For a long time I sat on the swing, my feet dangling while I watched the front door curious about what they said.

After what felt like an eternity to me, the church lady finally left.

As interested as I had been, I waited for a while before finding Mom in the living room and asking, "What did she say?"

Mom didn't answer me immediately, and I sat quietly while she reflected. After a bit, she reached over and stroked my sun-bleached hair and then looked absently away. At last, she turned and looked right into my eyes. "Laura, she had a little girl a long time ago."

"How long ago?" I questioned.

"About 20 years ago, but her little girl only lived to be ten years old. She had something wrong with her, and she wasn't even able to hold her head up straight." Mom tilted her head sideways to show me how the girl's head had rested on her shoulder because she wasn't strong enough to hold it up straight.

"What'd she look like? Did she have red hair like her mom?"

"Maybe, her mom didn't show me a picture, but she did say she was really cute and sweet."

"What was her name, Mom?" I wished with all my heart I could have known the girl who had lived a long time ago and then died when she was still little like me.

"I don't know. I mean, I don't remember if she told me her name, but the girl's grandma thought it was terrible that her family allowed her to live with them. She thought the girl should have been put in an institution. The grandma would try to hide her from other people by locking her in the bedroom; but the mom — the lady from church — loved her daughter and wanted people to see her. Even though she died a long time ago, the mom still misses her a lot."

My heart felt like it would explode in compassion for the mom and her little girl, and I said, "Why Mom? Why wouldn't the grandma let people see her?"

"I guess the grandma was embarrassed."

"Embarrassed of the girl?" I questioned. *How strange to be embarrassed of your cute granddaughter,* I thought.

"We will never be embarrassed of Berkeley, will we Mom?"

"No, we won't!" she said. "We will love him a lot."

Not until I became an adult myself did I comprehend what occurred during that visit. The lady showed my mom that loving Berkeley was the most natural thing in the whole world, and time and challenges would not change how much she already loved him.

Oddly, no one in our family can remember the name of the lady who came to visit. A few weeks later she and her husband moved away. We never knew why they came or why they left. Since our town barely earned a dot on the map, I have never come up with a good reason for them to have come to Soap Lake except that God brought them for us. Perhaps she was our angel unaware.

Although our pastor who had come with good intentions had not known what to say, the women in our church did, and they did what women throughout the ages have done. When Berkeley finally came home, they stood in line to hold him, talked about feeding schedules and sleep patterns, worried with Mom about his cough, and threw us the biggest baby shower I had ever seen.

With the rich aroma of coffee hanging in the air and sugary frosting on our lips, Amy and I took our places beside Mom in front of a table overloaded with gifts – so many gifts that some had to be stacked on the floor. One of the ladies suggested maybe Amy and I would like to help unwrap the presents.

"Slow down, don't open them so fast," implored Mom over and over, but in our excitement and with the ladies, who sat in folding chairs around the perimeter of the fellowship hall urging us on, we could not slow down. Tiny outfits, rattles, booties, hats, sleepers, toys, hand-made blankets, and every other baby thing imaginable came out of those beautifully wrapped packages.

"Look," Amy squealed as she tore off the wrapping paper from an orange rubber Kanga and her baby Roo.

"That's for bath time," Mom said as she reached down and pressed Kanga's side until the toy squeaked at us.

"Ah, cute," I held bibs up for everyone to see.

We could hardly wait to get home that evening to show Dad and our brothers all the wonderful things our friends had given to us.

I now know the greatest gifts given that night were not tangible but were instead the gifts of love, acceptance and concern. We would need those memories to see us through difficult conversations in the coming years. Although many people understood our deep abiding love for Berkeley, a few persisted in believing he came as a burden.

One evening I overheard my parents talking. Dad stood at the kitchen sink, all six feet and four inches of him, and he sounded upset.

"Mr. Hanson told me again today, 'The good thing is he won't live to be very old.' He insists on telling me that same stupid thing at least once a week."

"What did you say back to him?" Mom sounded concerned.

"It always catches me off guard. Each time he says it I feel so sad, but today it just made me angry. I told him, 'We love him! We don't want him to die!'"

I thought I heard Dad mutter, "Stupid man," but it might have been my imagination.

Those early years of Berkeley's life occurred long ago, but through the years I have reflected on the red—haired lady and her daughter versus the way most people treated our Berkeley. By the time he was born, times had already begun to change. Our extended family and friends embraced Berkeley with warmth and love.

When people told us, "He'll be such a blessing," we knew they viewed him as we did, a beautiful baby we wanted to keep in our home. Many people probably did not know what else to say, but we loved them for loving

Berkeley with us. Their acceptance, not pity, gave the encouragement needed.

HELP SECTION – WHAT DO I SAY?

Parents

Information and support groups exist now for nearly every kind of disability. However, the initial news is monumental for any parent and causes fear.

Friends/Acquaintances

1. Saying something is important. You cannot ignore the situation, but everyone reacts differently to the news that they have a disabled child. No matter what, this is a game changer for the family. Start by asking a neutral question such as, "How are you doing?"
2. Listen to the answer and watch body language. This will help you know what to say next.
3. Ask if you can do anything to help? Make specific suggestions about what you could do.
   a. Do you need me to watch your other children while you make visits to the hospital or get some sleep?
   b. Can I make you a meal?

4. Convey your concern for any health problems that may accompany the handicap.
5. Tell the parents you can't wait to meet the baby.
6. When you see the baby, compliment him or her. "He is darling." or "She is so cute."
7. If you always stick your foot in your mouth or suffer from extreme shyness, a hug from one woman to another conveys a lot of what you can't put into words. It can say, "I love you." or "I know you're hurting." or "I care but don't know what to say."

What are some Dos and Don'ts?

- Do send a card of congratulations.
- Do give a gift or throw a baby shower.
- Do assume the parents love their new baby.
- Do allow the parents to express their emotions.
- Do admire the baby.
- Don't send a sympathy card.
- Don't tell the parents how sorry you are!

Chapter 5

Valentine's Day

On February 14, 1980, I woke to the unmistakable sound of first Leigh and then Amy throwing up. I rolled out of bed and padded across the carpeted bedroom. Stepping onto the cold linoleum in the hallway, I pushed the bathroom door open just in time for Amy to stand up and stumble toward me. She looked terribly sick, and I almost asked her if she wanted me to take her temperature. Since we used the thermometer primarily for determining whether someone was really and truly ill, I decided to skip it. The smell and her miserable face confirmed she wasn't faking it.

Unfortunately for both Leigh and Amy, Mom and Dad had left for Seattle early that morning. Needing to sign paperwork for the new property they had just bought, they had talked about making the trip there and back in one day, but Grandpa and Grandma had urged them to spend the night with friends. "The kids will be fine," they encouraged. "We'll be right here, and it'd be good for you to get away."

I headed into Berky's room. Even though the doctors had done a good job repairing the hole between Berkeley's esophagus and windpipe, it would never work properly. Sleeping on a slope kept him from choking in the night, and his mattress inclined steeply. A cloth harness kept him from sliding to the bottom of the crib.

Berkeley smiled and cooed at me, and I leaned over his bed and asked, "How are you, Honey Bunch?" He reached his arms to me, and I pulled him out of bed. Happy as usual, he jabbered while I changed his diaper and put him into a clean onesie. "You get to spend the day with Grandma, Lucky Boy." I kissed his sweet little nose, and he leaned his mouth against my cheek and gave me a slobber kiss.

"Are you ready?" Ethan hollered.

"We're coming," I yelled back.

Ethan held the door for me and then let it crash closed behind us as I stepped onto the back porch. Flipping a blanket over Berkeley's head, I hugged him close to my chest to protect him from the chilled winter morning. Our breath made misty clouds that hung in the air for an instant before disappearing against sunshine already lighting a brilliant, clear blue sky. The three of us hurried across 50 yards of sandy, rocky ground separating the two houses; and since my arms were full of baby, Ethan banged on our grandparent's back door to announce our arrival. Not waiting for them to come to the door, we let ourselves in; and the warmth of their home enveloped us.

Grandpa had moved the old highchair into the kitchen, and I deposited Berkeley in it glad to let capable Grandma take over his care. Although we loved our grandma immensely, breakfast could be a study in disappointment. Trying not to think about it too much, I quickly ate my bowl of rapidly cooling cream of wheat, a skin of congealed cereal already covering the top. Thinking she had done something special for us, Grandma had added some home dried raisins in the cereal; but to my nine-year old eyes, they looked like giant bugs.

If breakfast left me disappointed, the Valentine's party at school made up for everything. We ate cupcakes, cookies, and handfuls of candy and washed it all down with generous portions of red Kool-Aid. Seemed that every mom and teacher in the school had contributed some sugary treat. At recess we played Crack the Whip, and Red Rover, and Simon Says; and then we came back inside and devoured more. No one cared how much we ate, but finally my aching stomach reminded me of sick siblings at home. Feeling badly that Leigh and Amy had to miss out, I wrapped a handful of candy in a napkin and tucked it in my jumper pocket. I planned on surprising them with a tiny bit of the party when they felt better. Then I went and sat at my desk. I had a strange little ache in the back of my head.

By the time Ethan and I got home, Leigh and Amy had moved out of their bedrooms and lay on the living room floor playing a game of Monopoly.

"We're supposed to go over to Grandma's for supper," Amy said when I showed her the candy I had smuggled home. "But I'm not very hungry."

"Ugh, I'm not hungry either," I said.

"Maybe you will be by supper time," Ethan said. "Do you want to go over and get Berky so Grandma can have a break for a while?"

"I guess," I said as I heaved myself up from the couch. "I feel sort of awful. Maybe I ate too much candy."

I trudged outside, and a minute later I rapped on the back door.

"Come in," I heard Grandma's cheerful invitation.

"Oh, Laura," she said looking up from a heart shaped cake she had generously smothered in creamy pink icing. "You're just in time to lick the frosting bowl."

On any other day, I would have been thrilled. Instead, I felt a wave of nausea roll over me. I hated to let her down so I swirled my fingers unenthusiastically around the edge of the bowl and licked the sweetness.

Maybe Mom is right, and you can eat too much sugar, I thought.

"Look," Grandma said, "I made it in the shape of a heart. If you want, you can decorate it with red hots."

I did not want to see another piece of candy let alone eat a big old slice of cake.

"Do you want me to take Berky home for a little while?" I asked.

"Oh, he's been no problem at all," Grandma said waving toward the living room where Berkeley lay on a clean blanket. "He's been really quiet this afternoon."

I picked him up and kissed him, but he didn't give me another slobbery kiss, just laid his head on my shoulder.

"Supper is about ready if you want to go get your brothers and sister."

As I opened the back door, the same fresh air I had enjoyed in the morning met me; but now the 50 yards between the houses seemed like a mile. My body protested every step, and the soles of my shoes felt as heavy as concrete. My eyes burned in the sunlight; and by the time I opened the back door, I felt like I had to sit down. I headed straight for the couch and mumbled, "Grandma's ready for us."

"I'm tired," Amy said, "and I don't want to eat."

"That's okay," Ethan told her. "Just sit at the table. Grandma knows you've been sick."

During supper, my head began to throb, and my eyes felt scratchy and heavy.

I didn't want to admit what a pig I had made of myself at school. So, when Grandma, usually so conservative with portions of sweets, placed a huge slice of

cake on my plate, I determinedly shoved bites into my
mouth. She beamed at us, and we made a valiant effort
because we loved her, and she had made such a nice
surprise for us.

Then it hit me, the distinct notion that what I had
eaten would not stay down. Without even saying "excuse
me," I pushed my chair back from the table and ran for
the bathroom. By the time I finished, Ethan, already
hovering in the doorway entered and pushed me aside.
Berkeley began to cry; and when I picked him up, he
vomited down the side of my blouse. That set me off
again, and Grandma surveyed us with dejection.

"I'm sorry, Grandma," I said. Sheer willpower kept
me from throwing up again. I swallowed hard, but a
chill made my whole-body shudder. "It was such a pretty
cake," I finished lamely.

Grandpa had taken Berky from me and wiped him
off, but he handed him back when Ethan said we would
take him home and clean him up. "I think we'd all better
go home," Ethan's voice sounded scratchy and far away.

"Well, you kids call if you need anything," Grandma
said as we straggled out the back door. I am certain she
thought we had simply eaten too many sweets and would
go home and sleep it off.

Instead, we embarked on one of the most awful
nights of our young lives.

Amy and Leigh worn out from being sick in the morning promptly went to bed. Ethan, Berk, and I had just begun.

Ethan sat in the rocker, and I took the recliner. When I was about to vomit, I gasped, "Ethan, take him." We leaned towards each other, and I handed Berk off. Pulling the bucket close, I puked until my sides ached. Soon Ethan handed Berkeley back to me.

Sometime in the middle of the night, Leigh got out of bed and came out to check on us. "Why don't you put him in his crib?" he asked.

"We can't, he might choke on his vomit. He's got to be held upright." My stomach churned, and my face burned.

Leigh took Berkeley down the hall and changed his diaper and put him in clean pajamas before depositing him back into Ethan's arms.

I squinted across at Ethan, and his face was ashen and puffy.

"See Laura," he rasped, "if you put a bowl behind you for Berk, you barely have to move. Just lean back and let him throw up. Then lean forward and you can throw up into your own bucket."

I tried Ethan's method once and ended up with vomit all over my left shoulder which set off a new spasm of heaving.

Finally, we fell into a restless sleep. I remembered waking and looking over at Ethan with Berk perched on his shoulder. "Do you want me to take him again?" I whispered.

"Nah, it might wake him," and we both fell back into a feverish, restless sleep.

Somewhere in the night, Ethan gave him back to me, but I barely remembered it. *So this is what it's like to be a mother,* I thought. *Even when you're sick, you still have to take care of the children.*

Mom and Dad must have gotten up before daylight because it wasn't even mid-morning when they got home.

"Kids," Mom said taking in the sight and knowing without asking what had happened. "I'm so sorry. Oh, I'm so sorry."

How I loved her efficiency and the feel of Dad lifting Berkeley out of my arms and then having myself tucked into bed. And just like that, I became the child again. But my nurturing motherly side had awakened, and I was proud. I was proud that Ethan and I had kept Berkeley alive through the long night.

As I drifted off to sleep, a thought occurred to me that held me conscious for an instant before I gave into the heaviness of my eyelids. Berky had never cried during our horrible night. He had thrown up repeatedly, been passed back and forth, back and forth, and back and forth; but he never fussed or cried. *He's a tough baby,* I thought. *He knew we were sick too. What a good baby,* and then sleep claimed my worn-out little frame.

HELP SECTION

Parents

If you have other children, let them know from the beginning how much you value them as siblings. Praise and thank them for their help. Because a child with disabilities often does take extra care, this important step keeps them from feeling like they have become less important in the family structure.

Chapter 6
Full of Crackers

"Mom, where's Amy?" I had wandered into the kitchen and found Mom busily separating milk from cream. As usual, she had gotten up at dawn to milk the cow, and later in the day she would make butter. Mom never seemed to stop except for a short power nap in the afternoon.

"I think she's in my room reading to Berky."

"Okay," I said as I backed out of the kitchen. If I lingered, she would give me a job.

I found Amy, just as Mom said, sitting against the headboard of the bed with Berkeley beside her. A pile of pillows propped Berkeley into a sitting position. As I walked into the room, I asked, "What are you doing?"

"Shh," Amy replied, "I'm reading to Berky so he'll take a nap."

Berkeley cooed, made a fist, and poked it into his mouth. I picked up a burp cloth and wiped the slobber off his face.

"He doesn't look very sleepy to me."

"No, he isn't going to sleep very fast." She said it with a resigned timbre to her voice as if she had never expected him to fall asleep in the first place.

Feeling left out and not wanting to listen to Amy read about big trucks, green trucks, slow trucks, and fast trucks, I said, "Do you want to play school with him instead?"

"Sure," she said as she rolled off the edge of the bed. "I'll go get the animals."

A few minutes later, we moved to the living room; and instead of pillows, stuffed animals propped Berkeley into a sitting position.

"Now children," Amy said, "I'm going to tell you your ABCs, and Laura is going to hold them up for you to see."

"A is for apple."

Obediently I held up a flashcard with a picture of an apple and the letter A printed on it.

Berkeley babbled and clapped his hands together.

"B for Berkeley."

He smiled, and Amy gave him a kiss. At the same time, I stepped forward and gently pushed his tongue back into his mouth. His therapist told us that Berkeley could learn to hold his tongue in his mouth if we pushed it each time it lolled out. Amy and I had become the tongue police; and at first, we pressed his tongue with our fingers dozens of times in a day. After a couple of months, we no longer needed to push his tongue into his mouth. The muscles in his tongue grew strong with the constant reinforcement, and he naturally kept his mouth closed.

"C is for Cat."

Frosty the cat sauntered into the living room as if on cue, and I picked him up and held him close to Berkeley. "Isn't our kitty cat soft, Berkeley?"

His tiny hands batted at the silky fur.

"No Berkeley don't hit the kitty," I said as I captured his hands in mine. "Like this," and I helped him stroke Frosty instead. I released his hands, and he began batting again. "No," I said and helped him stroke.

Even though he didn't understand our ABC flash-cards, playing school with Berkeley became one of our favorite games. We kept busy with lots of activities completely unrelated to traditional schooling. We dressed him, danced with him, sang with him, kissed him; and when the stuffed animals failed to keep him upright and he toppled over, we helped him sit back up. As his muscles strengthened, he tumbled over less often. Amy and I noticed each bit of progress he made, and we cele-brated all his achievements. But we really wanted him to crawl because his therapist had told us that crawling was an important milestone to reach.

"I think it's time for snacks," Amy announced.

I headed to the kitchen where it was butter churning day again. Speaking up so Mom could hear over the sound of the electric churner's constant hum, I asked. "Mom, can we give Berky some crackers? We want to help him practice his reaching."

Mom furrowed her brow while she considered. "You can give him two. I don't want you to spoil his lunch."

Amy went to the cupboard and got the crackers while I placed Berkeley on his tummy. We held a cracker for him ever so slightly out of his reach. Pushing himself up with one arm, Berkeley reached for the cracker. When he could not quite grasp it, Amy held it closer; but Berkeley had already put his reaching arm down and now pushed hard against the floor and pulled himself toward the cracker.

"Did you see that?" We looked at each other in amazement and then began jumping up and down and yelling at each other. "Did you see that? Did you see that?"

Mom came into the living room to see what the commotion was all about. "He's crawling Mom; he's really crawling." I could not keep my voice quiet.

Berkeley still on his tummy arched his back so his head and arms came off the floor. One hand shoved a cracker into his mouth, and the other waved in the air. When he finished, we held another cracker just out of his reach. He pulled himself forward until his fingers closed on it.

Mom didn't exactly jump up and down like Amy and I did, but her body seemed to emit electricity as her hands clasped together, released, rose in the air in a silent cheer and then came together again in a noiseless clap. Ignoring the two-cracker rule, Mom grabbed an entire sleeve of them out of the cupboard. Again and again we bribed him with crackers and then cheered as he moved forward.

"It's not really crawling," Mom told us as she held a cracker in front of him. "He's scooting. He has to be on his knees to crawl, but he is scooting."

When Dad and the boys came in from the shop, we gave Berkeley more crackers, and the whole family stood around cheering for him while he scooted around the living room floor following a cracker trail.

When we finally sat down to lunch, Berkeley did not eat a thing. He was full of crackers.

HELP SECTION

Parents

When Berkeley started elementary school, his teacher told us that Berkeley's progress far surpassed other children with Down syndrome who possessed higher cognitive skills. They attributed his success to his social skills. "If we place him in a classroom with typically developing children and they are practicing writing, he will take out a piece of paper and try to write too. He is very good at mimicking what those around him are doing. No one walking into the classroom would notice that he has Down syndrome unless they were to look at him closely. We can tell he has been highly socialized."

First time parents are often terrified their baby will break. Because so many Down syndrome babies have undergone extensive surgeries, this fear is magnified. But God made their little bones soft and flexible just like other babies, and they will not break as easily as you might suspect. If you have other children, encourage them to play with the baby. If this is your only child, fight the fear and start having friends over who have gentle children. Let them haul around that little bundle of joy.

Not only did Berkeley benefit from all the play time, but Amy and I became great assets to our parents. Here are a few pointers:

- Discipline is necessary.
    - √ Pushing Berkeley's tongue back into his mouth was not unkind; it was a labor of love.
    - √ Berkeley had to be told "No" for a multitude of things, and sometimes the "No" had to be reinforced. All children need boundaries.
- Socialize your baby – the more the better.
    - √ As much as possible, treat this child just as you would any child.

√ Talk to your baby.

√ Read to your baby.

√ Socialization helps your child adjust to the world.

√ Socialization helps everyone else adjust to your child!

Friends/Acquaintances

- Physical contact is important; however, if you are not family
    - √ Ask permission before touching any baby.
    - √ Do not touch any baby if you have a cold or even think you might be sick. Many special needs babies have compromised immune systems, and something as simple as a cold may become life threatening.

Chapter 7

Berkeley Goes to Church

"I'm about to give up grocery shopping," Mom told us one afternoon. "I had two complete strangers stop me today and tell me 'For goodness' sake, get that baby to a doctor.'"

Scar tissue from his early surgeries had left Berkeley with a deep, hacking cough — the kind you would expect from a chain smoker, and people everywhere stopped to stare and give dirty looks.

"That's so rude! They should mind their own business."

"I can't blame them, Laura. I'd be thinking the same thing; but when I tried to explain why he coughs like that, one woman got super huffy and wouldn't even hear what I had to say. She was sure he had pneumonia. It was obvious both women thought I was a terrible mother."

Like so many things most parents take for granted, Mom had a long argument with herself about whether or not to place Berkeley in the church nursery. Never having been a fan of dropping her children off for some-one else to watch, she secretly wished to keep him with her in the service. The debate raged in her head. Afraid his cough would be too disruptive in church, she finally opted to place him in the nursery. A short time later, she stopped when one of the older ladies took her aside and confidentially told her Berkeley's coughing fits scared the nursery workers. "We love him, but some of the ladies are afraid he'll die when he starts coughing."

From then on, Mom kept Berkeley with her in the worship service; and if he started coughing hard, she took him to the foyer. As she left the auditorium, our friends and church family gave her looks of concern.

Even as a fragile baby, his magnetic personality captured the hearts and affection of everyone he met. Surrounded by love, Berkeley's body gradually became stronger and his cough a little less raucous. As the terrifying cough lessened, he started to try other sounds and even words.

When Ethan, as a baby, learned to pat his mouth while making sound, Mom and Dad were thrilled new parents and thought this accomplishment was wonderful and amazing. By the time Amy came along, they quite expected she would learn to do the same. But when Berkeley learned that if he would say "Bahhhhhhhhh" and Amy and I would pat his mouth to create a discon-nected "bah, bah, bah," first time parents could not have been prouder. Four adoring siblings clapped for him and told him he was the smartest, cutest baby alive.

Berkeley loved the attention and would make the sound the instant we tapped his lips

On a particularly hot Sunday evening, someone propped all the windows and doors open to let a little air into the stuffy church auditorium. Meanwhile, a guest speaker droned on and on. Wondering if church would never end, I snuck peaks at the clock at the back of the room and watched it slowly tick past closing time, 10 minutes, 30 minutes, 40 minutes. Bored, Berkeley began to sing a soft little "Bahhhhh."

Mom covered his mouth and whispered, "Shhh." She turned him on her lap, and he repeated, "Bahhhh."

Absent-mindedly, she covered his mouth and held her fingers softly against his lips. The sound stopped. She released and shifted him again.

He said, "Bahhh," and she covered his mouth.

By this time, not needing a lot to distract us from the long-winded speaker, the rest of the family leaned slightly forward in their seats and stared down the pew at them.

Without thinking Mom covered Berkeley's mouth again and released as soon as he grew silent. "Bah, bah, bah." He smiled and waved his arms.

I looked past Mom and could see Dad's mouth purse into a hard line. His eyes twinkled when he nudged Ethan with his elbow and tilted his head toward Berkeley. Amy whispered into my ear, "He's bahing." Beside me, Leigh began to shake with laughter, and Mom finally came to her senses. With a startled look, she pulled her hand away from Berkeley's mouth, and then the whole family lost it. Right there in the middle of church and during that unending sermon, we shook with laughter. I tried to breathe without making a sound, but Amy covered her mouth and giggled out loud. Finally, I lifted my head to gasp for air and found myself staring straight into the speaker's eyes. His lips parted, but he had ceased to speak. Our eyes locked and then with resignation in his voice, he announced, "Let us close in prayer."

Berkeley's popularity kept growing with our small congregation; and one evening while friends stood around visiting after church, Dad casually laid Berkeley on his stomach and said, "Watch this trick!"

With his face, belly, and legs flat on the blanket, Berkeley began to move his legs until they stuck out like a T from his hips. His legs continued to move in a circular motion until they pointed forward by his head. He still lay completely flat, face down on the floor; and a little gasp of amazement rose from the attentive audience. Then he used his arms to push his torso up, and there he sat gazing up at us.

"He started sitting up this week," I said bouncing up and down in excitement.

"How is he even able to do that?" our rapt audience kept asking.

"The doctor said it is not uncommon for Down syndrome children to have loose joints that make things like this possible. He'll do it all day," Dad said as he picked Berkeley up and laid him on his tummy again. Sensing he was the center of attention, Berkeley swung his legs around and again pushed himself into a sitting position. He smiled and waved his hands at us.

Mrs. Friend stood looking at him with awe and said, "Do it again. I can't believe it. Please, have him do it again." Over and over, Dad placed Berkeley face down on the floor, and we watched while he swung his legs around until he could gaze up at the giants standing over him.

Several months later when Dad received a job offer in Seattle, we had to leave that wonderful support group behind. From the day Berkeley had been born, the good souls in that church had prayed for him, showered him with gifts, and had welcomed him into a circle of love. They treated him like a wanted child and never considered him a mistake.

We missed our friends when we moved, but Berkeley quickly helped us make new ones who, like the old ones, celebrated his every landmark accomplishment ten-fold.

Our new church family opened their arms to him and loved to watch him develop and grow too. Often, on Sunday mornings, several people tiptoed to our pew after the service to see if Berkeley was still sleeping. The fascination of seeing him asleep never grew old. Starting in an upright sitting position, he would let his face drop until his chubby cheek rested on the pew and directly between his legs which V-d out in front of him. In that position he would spend a restful 30 minutes until the pastor wrapped up the message and one of us picked him up off the pew.

After church people loved to hold Berkeley and play with him. Happy and growing stronger and healthier, he had even started saying words; but when Berkeley turned two, he still could not walk.

An older friend expressed her concern to Mom many times. "Maybe you should buy him a walker," she pestered.

"No," Mom answered trying to be gracious and explaining for what seemed like the thousandth time. "The doctor says he must learn to crawl properly before we push him to walk. If he doesn't crawl first, he'll miss out on developing some of his finer motor skills. It's okay though. He'll make it. He's starting to switch over from his scooting to almost crawling, and we've got lots of time."

As they often did, the teens lined up to see Berkeley; and Ethan grabbed him and headed to the back of the church with a small crowd following. Soon cheers from all the big kids could be heard as Berkeley performed his unique sitting up skills. One of the girls had snuck graham crackers out of the nursery, and she began bribing Berkeley to scoot along the floor.

"Look," Leigh yelled. "He's got his knees under him. He's crawling; he's actually crawling this time!" Suddenly the crowd expanded to include grownups, and Berkeley distracted by the attention sat and stared up at everyone. "Give him another cracker," someone shouted; and soon to the delight of dozens of friends, Berkeley crawled across the church foyer.

HELP SECTION

Parents

1. Be a proud parent. We talked openly about Berkeley and his special needs, and that made it easy for people to celebrate with us whenever he accomplished something big or small.
2. Don't be too private. Because we did not act secretive or ashamed of his Down syndrome, people did not feel awkward around him or us.
3. Be approachable! We were thankful that someone who loved our family and Berkeley was honest enough to approach us about the nursery situation. Reassured that he was welcome in the church service eased Mom's concern about the noise he made, and the ladies no longer had to worry that he might die on their watch.

Friends/Acquaintances

Do not push your opinion onto the parents. My parents had consulted with therapists and doctors. The experts of the time cautioned them not to push Berkeley to walk until he had learned to crawl. Although our friend meant well by repeatedly suggesting we get a walker, she unnecessarily added to the concerns we already had about him learning to walk. And Berkeley did walk. Shortly after he passed his second birthday, not only had he learned to walk but was also potty trained. We had a lot more challenges to face, but with patience and love, we overcame them all.

Chapter 8
The Cool Kid

"**I**s Berkeley coming to the game?" A good-looking high school boy hollered at Ethan as he ran past me. "Yeah, my mom should be here pretty soon – before the game starts."

On the sidelines of the soccer field, I watched the team go through their warmup drills while keeping one eye on the parking lot.

When we arrived at our new school, we felt nervous and backwards – kids from a farm now plopped into the city. We didn't have expensive clothes or haircuts; but Berkeley, the most different of all became an instant hit.

When Mom picked us up in our old, rust colored station wagon, Berkeley stood in the passenger seat waving and smiling to everyone who walked past the car. Within days, girls made a beeline for Berkeley after school. They pulled him through the passenger window so they could hold and play with him. The guys, a little more macho, came by to exchange high fives with him.

When Ethan got his driver's license and Mom no longer came to school with Berkeley, our friends missed him and asked about him. Game day became their chance to catch up and see him in person.

"Hey, Berkeley's here!" I heard someone yell.

Taking a quick break, Ethan and Leigh jogged to the edge of the field and waited for him. Not only able to walk, he could now run, albeit his gate was slightly off beat and awkward – a bit like an unbalanced windmill. Berkeley rushed to his big brothers who picked him up and swung him high into the air. The rest of the team circled around and reached in to pat him on the back before the coach yelled for them to "get back over here."

Coach Schukar assigned a drill to the team before sneaking to the sidelines. Bending down to Berkeley's level, he smothered Berkeley's tiny hand in his own large one.

When the game started and the other spectators started to cheer, Berkeley ran up and down the sidelines, his eyes never leaving his big brothers. When Ethan intercepted the ball, everyone heard a tiny voice yelling "Eedah."

Scooping him up in my arms, I began to yell with him, "Ethan, Ethan" until everyone yelled with us. Berkeley's arms circled my neck, and he planted slobbery kisses on my cheek which dried in the crisp autumn air.

As I set him back on the ground, Leigh's foot connected and sent the soccer ball flying. Teammates cheered for Leigh, but Berkeley, unable to pronounce his Ls yelled "Gheeee."

As the moms and spectators started laughing, I heard one of my brothers' buddies say, "Ethan and Leigh's little brother is so cool."

His popularity did not end with our friends or the people we knew personally. Wherever we took Berkeley, people seemed attracted to him. Perfect strangers would take an interest in him and his well-being.

Berkeley loved to go to sporting events, and one day we took him to see the Mariners, Seattle's professional baseball team. Unfortunately, when we entered the stadium, we discovered he had an interesting phobia. Whether it was the throng of people, the way the seats were set into steep rows that seemed to drop off into nowhere, or the noise, he was scared — so frightened that he insisted on sitting on someone's lap with his face pressed into their chest.

As the game dragged along, people behind us and directly in front of us tried to coax him into watching the game. They worried and fussed over him, but he kept his face buried in Dad's shirt.

Then someone behind us, a stranger before the game, draped a pennant over his head. Slowly he turned around, and with his tiny fingers gripping Dad's pant leg, he peeked out from behind the banner. These people who did not even know our names whispered, pointed, and smiled. And then one of the players hit a home run. As the crowd exploded, Berkeley pushed his fear aside.

He let go of his handful of denim and raised his hands in the air to celebrate. As the roar in the stadium died away, he once again grabbed hold of the loose fabric of Dad's jeans while he hid his face behind the banner. Around us, people continued to clap. But they were not looking at the baseball diamond; they cheered for Berkeley. They recognized that in a small way, he had conquered a bit of his fear.

HELP SECTION

Parents

Every Down syndrome person will function at a different level because the variability of the disability from child to child. Comparing one child to another is not a good idea with typically developing children, but this is especially true with Down syndrome. Instead, focus on each person as an individual and celebrate all their successes – no matter how big or small.

Facebook and the internet are full of testimonials of high functioning people with Down syndrome right now. I think their accomplishments are amazing, and I celebrate them. But I have also caught myself feeling defensive because Berkeley does not function at that same high level.

I even worry that some people reading this book may feel sad because their child's disability may be more severe than Berkeley's disability and does not allow for as much social interaction, but each child is God's special creation and has purpose and value.

Friends/Acquaintances

Know that it can mean the world to the family when you take an interest. Don't worry if the person can't respond. Tell them you are glad to see them. Pat them on the shoulder or shake their hand.

When you do not know what to say to someone and are afraid they will not be able to respond or even able to acknowledge you, you can address them and the family in a general way by saying something like, "Hey, I'm glad you could come to the game tonight." In this non-invasive way, you provide the parents or caregivers with assurance that you accept them. You do not need to push beyond this. If the parents feel comfortable, they will engage with you further. For personal reasons, they may not wish to talk further.

Never ask questions such as "What is wrong with your child or what disease do they have?" Certain disabilities such as cerebral palsy may affect the body profoundly but not the mind. Imagine being locked in a body that does not allow you to move freely and gives you the appearance of being mentally limited, but you have a sharp mind. If someone were to talk down to you or ask demeaning questions, imagine how you would feel.

On the off chance that you encounter someone who does not accept your friendliness, know that they are the exception not the rule. Do not let one bad experience color your future actions.

Chapter 9
The Chicken Herder

"Mom, do you know where my term paper is?" Slight panic edged Ethan's question.

"Where'd you leave it?" Mom asked without bothering to turn away from the sink.

"On the end of the counter. I know I left it right there?"

Mom turned around and cast a puzzled look at the counter. "No, I haven't seen it."

"You don't think Berk moved it — do you?" Ethan's voice trailed off. This was more than a slight possibility. Berkeley loved to pack things; and if history had any bearing, our future held full-blown panic. But first came the pleading.

"Did you take my paper, Berkeley?"

"Where did you put Ethan's paper? Berkeley, did you move Ethan's paper?"

"Ya, ya papah." Berkeley nodded his head up and down. Now seven years old, he had become more mobile but still struggled with his verbal skills.

71

"Where did you put Ethan's paper?" Mom held Berkeley's head gently in her hands and spoke while she looked directly into his eyes.

"Ya, ya papah." Berkeley picked up a piece of mail lying on the table and held it up to Mom.

Mom sighed. "Everybody start looking. We have ten minutes before we need to be out the door."

Like a bomb squad, we spread throughout the house. In the middle of the living room floor, someone dumped and searched the contents of a duffle bag, his favorite thing to pack. Berkeley did not limit his creativity when it came to finding ways to make our stuff disappear. The previous week we found Amy's gym clothes in a grocery bag behind the couch.

All through the house you could hear drawers slide open and shut and closet doors close with a thud. Someone checked the back porch and then the front porch. We looked under beds and behind chairs; and when all hope seemed lost, we prepared to leave for school. Ethan's head drooped in defeat.

We all looked on in sympathy, and then from the back of the house we heard Amy yell, "I found it! I found it!" Emerging from her bedroom, she held her canvas school bag in one hand while the other triumphantly waved Ethan's paper over her head.

"Where?" Ethan asked.

"In my bag, on the end of the bed."

Berkeley smiled, "Ya, ya papah."

"Berkeley, you shouldn't move Ethan's papers," Mom's voice sounded strained and stern, but Berkeley seemed confused by the terseness in her voice.

"I think he thought he was trying to be helpful," I said. "He did put it in a school bag."

"I would have flunked that class. How would it look for me to flunk my first college course?" Ethan grabbed the paper and glared at Berkeley.

"It's kind of cute when he packs toys in our lunches though," Leigh said. "Yesterday he packed a truck in my lunch and a plastic horse in Laura's."

"Everyone waits for us to open our lunches so they can see what Berky packed," I said. "I think he just wants us to have fun at school."

"Leigh wasn't so happy when Berkeley stuffed a bunch of nuts and bolts into the axle of the truck he was working on," Ethan said. "Anyway, I've got to go. I'm practically late already, but that kid needs something to do."

That evening, feeling significantly calmer, we again discussed the packing problem.

"Do you remember when Berky took the keys to the tractor?" Amy asked. "That was pretty bad."

We grew silent as we thought about Berkeley. Finding a toy in your lunch bag at school was cute; but at one time or another, we had all suffered from his habit of packing and hiding things. A few months earlier, Dad had to buy a new pair of glasses. We assumed Berkeley had hidden them away somewhere, and we never did find the keys to the tractor.

"I'm sorry kids," Mom said. "I know it's frustrating, but he really doesn't understand what he's doing."

"He needs chores!" Amy said emphatically. And we realized she was right. He needed, like all kids, something to keep himself occupied.

Keeping the chickens out of the garden became Berkeley's first official job, and he took on that responsibility with a stamina and perseverance amazing to us all.

The chickens had scratched out all the early vegetables; so, Mom gave Berkeley a long stick and told him not to let the chickens in the garden. In the afternoons, when we came home from school and started up the long driveway to the house, we could see Berkeley shepherding the chickens away from the garden. In the beginning he worried them so much they stopped laying eggs; but after a bit, they must have grown used to him running around the edge of the garden shooing them away. Eventually, they stopped venturing into the garden altogether; and we had to find new jobs for Berkeley.

Even with the chicken job, he still had occasional relapses with the packing; but we learned to keep important papers out of reach.

By the time he turned ten, he had discovered a splitting maul; and splitting wood became the great love of his life. I spent a lot of time trying to convince Mom it was too dangerous, but after a while I gave up. He was good at it, and he loved splitting wood. Every year he grew stronger and healthier; and eventually, he split all our wood and wood for the neighbors too.

HELP SECTION

Parents

Distinguishing between what needs punishment and what needs redirection in a child with disabilities takes a great amount of wisdom. I only remember one time where my parents seriously punished Berkeley.

As we built our house, Berkeley kept entering the construction zone and climbing ladders. Dad would come down a ladder to get a tool and then turn around to see that Berkeley had climbed to a dangerously high rung. Unsure of whether Berkeley understood him, Dad repeatedly scolded, lectured, and forbid Berkeley to climb the ladders; but Berkeley either did not understand or refused to obey.

When the basement walls towered over the concrete floor, Dad rounded a corner to see Berkeley perched atop a ladder high above the cement. Fearful that Berkeley would fall to his death, Dad finally had to administer something harsher than words. None of us wanted Dad to punish Berkeley, but he had to protect him from harm. Berkeley never climbed the ladder again.

All children need boundaries, but the challenge is to make discipline productive. If the child does not understand the reason for punishment, it will be detrimental. Dad made sure Berky understood the punishment was for climbing the ladder and used extreme caution to make certain he did not cross a line and become harsh.

His packing problem had additional challenges because of the many variables. Berkeley found so many things to pick up and move, and we could not possibly restrict him from touching everything. Keeping him busy with other projects helped alleviate the problem.

Chapter 10

I Said "No!"

Our church friends adored Berkeley from the beginning. As soon as he stepped into the foyer each Sunday, they mobbed him with hugs, kisses, presents, and lots of candy.

The loving attention people gave Berkeley pleased our family, and Berkeley found joy in accepting it. But we wondered what would happen as he grew older and bigger. Those bear hugs he gave people and the kisses he so generously passed out to everyone, would they be welcome when he grew into a man and was no longer a cute little boy?

We launched a no hugs, no kissing campaign. Gently I took Berkeley's face in my hands. I often did this when I wanted him to focus and pay attention. With his limited hearing, he could see my lips forming the words. This method also kept him from being distracted while I spoke. "You can't hug and kiss people at church Berkeley. Remember NO kissing."

From its conception, the plan failed. Although we convinced Berkeley he shouldn't kiss anyone outside of his immediate family, our friends didn't comply with the no hug rule.

When we walked through the church doors, women threw their arms wide open and Berkeley stepped into them.

"Well, I don't feel like I've been to church if I don't get my Berkeley hug," one lady told Mom as she tried to explain why we didn't want Berkeley hugging people.

"Could you at least not kiss him?" we reasoned.

In the end, we helped Berkeley and our church members understand a balanced but more complicated set of rules.

1. Only kiss Mom, Dad, and your sisters.
2. Only hug people who ask to be hugged.
3. Shake hands with all men except your brothers... you can hug your brothers.

Berkeley developed a sixth sense about who he should hug. Even with his limited abilities, he learned to read body language and simply shook hands with the non-huggers. I feared he wouldn't distinguish between friends of the family and strangers, but he understood those dynamics as well, politely shaking hands with people he met outside of our inner circle. Eventually we didn't need to worry about him kissing and hugging people anymore, and he remained the darling of the church.

On the way home from church one Sunday afternoon, Berkeley showed me a Snickers bar someone had given him.

"Oh Berkeley, can I have a bite?"

"No."

His response surprised me completely. Berkeley always shared with me.

"Please can I have a bite?" I pled.

"No!"

"Please! Just a little bite. I won't take much."

"NO!"

"Really? Berkeley, please, please just one little bite."

Suddenly he grabbed my face with both hands and turned my face to look fully into his. Firmly, he told me, "I...SAID...NO!"

I burst out laughing and stopped asking him for his candy.

As we taught Berkeley boundaries, we had to learn some of our own. As he grew older, he wanted more independence and a sense of his own belongings.

When his nieces and nephews were little, they invaded his room scattering toys all over the floor. After having his room destroyed several weeks in a row on Sunday afternoons, he started shutting the door and locking it so they could not play in his bedroom.

At first this seemed selfish and unlike him; but when we looked at it from his perspective, it made sense. Berkeley loved order and cleanliness. As adults, we did too; so we sent the children to his room so we wouldn't have to look at the mess. Consequently, every Sunday afternoon Berkeley lost his room and not for just a few minutes but for the entire day.

We designated a new play area, and when the children came to play, Berkeley helped them drag the big bins of toys to the new play area. As soon as they stopped scattering toys throughout his space, he welcomed them back into his room.

HELP SECTION

Even after growing up with him, I often find myself lapsing into treating Berkeley like a small child with no privacy or rights to make his own decisions. Of course, this stems from him not always being able to make good decisions on his own; but it is vitally important to give each person a sense of privacy and control of their lives and possessions.

Chapter 11

Welcome Home

As I pulled up in front of the house and switched off the engine, I heard the lyrics from Berkeley's favorite musical blasting from the living room.

Berkeley followed the same routine every afternoon. Get home from school, eat a snack, watch the *Little Mermaid* with the volume deafeningly loud, and wait for his siblings and dad to get home from their respective places of school or work.

For years Mom had asked doctors to test Berkeley's hearing. "I don't think he can hear," she told them.

"We don't have a good way of testing him for hearing loss," they replied. And then one day when Mom had given up asking about his ears, a doctor announced, "His hearing is deficient, really quite a severe loss; and it will only get worse because it's an issue with the nerves."

"What about hearing aids?" she asked.

"Oh definitely," he responded, "We'll try them, but there are certain sounds like "s" and "f" he'll never be able to distinguish no matter how strong the hearing aids are. Unfortunately, this was detected so late that he's missed out on key years of speech development."

For years I struggled with frustration over the previous doctors' dismissive attitudes when Mom had tried to convince them that Berkeley had a hearing loss. Many people with Down syndrome experience some trouble speaking clearly because God shaped their tongues and palates a little differently than the way He shaped most other people's mouths. Berkeley struggled even more with his speech because he never could differentiate between certain consonants.

At some point I came to accept his hearing loss as just another part of who he is. Feeling bad about it could not change the progress he had or had not made. We could only move forward; and even after he got hearing aids, he hated wearing them. So often, his movies or music deafened the rest of us.

I cranked the window up and leaned over to grab my purse from the passenger seat. As I glanced back at the house, I saw Mom through the picture window turn and gesture toward the living room. A few seconds later, Berkeley appeared on the front step. Face beaming, he held his arms wide open. "Honey!" he shouted.

Never did I feel as loved as I did on those days arriving home from work. The problems of the day melted away as I ran up the front porch stairs to claim my hug. As I entered the house, I waved at Mom; and no matter how many times I had seen the same movie, I flopped onto the couch and watched part of it with him. As each family member arrived home, Berkeley hit pause, giving my ears a welcome rest, so he could give them the same welcome home reception.

HELP SECTION

Parents

You will advocate for your child and consider it your job to do so. However, sometimes you must accept that you cannot control certain things. At times, you will even have to live with the knowledge that in hindsight, you could have done better.

Learn to accept that you can't go back in time and that you will lose some battles no matter how much effort you pour into them.

Resolve to love your child and move forward doing your best. Although giving them advantages and opportunities are great gifts, loving your child provides more than all the other advantages in the world. Love trumps opportunities and accomplishments!

Chapter 12

The Green Truck

Mom and I stood at the sink cleaning and slicing cucumbers for pickles when Berkeley came wandering through the kitchen. He stopped to hug us both.

"What're you gonna do now?" I asked him.

He bent slightly over at the waist, made a dribbling motion with his right hand and then straightened up as his right arm pushed against an invisible ball.

"Basketball," he said.

"Have fun!" I yelled as the back door slammed behind him. I dried my hands and moved to the window to watch. He disappeared briefly into the garage and then emerged with his basketball. With remarkable precision, Berkeley sank basket after basket from various angles in the driveway.

When Mom came to the window, I stepped over to make room, and we stood watching him, silent in our own thoughts.

As I stood next to my mother, both of us filled with love and hope for Berkeley, an empathetic understanding crept into my mind; and with it, I crossed the threshold from childhood to adulthood. I realized for the first time that, when Berkeley was born, Mom had not been so much older than I was now. Capable, in charge, Mom who always knew what to do and how to do it had one day received news that changed her present and future.

How did she reconcile her hopes and dreams for the baby she had carried for nine months to the news that he would not grow up to be the same as other children? Surely it must have rocked her to the core, but she had never let me see that side of her. And I had never asked. In my childish self-absorption, I never considered her emotions, struggles, and disappointments. With the dawning of this unexpected comprehension, I wanted to hear, out loud, the inner thoughts Mom must have had and kept hidden from the rest of the world.

"Mom, what is the hardest thing for you about having Berkeley?" I blurted out.

Mom placed her index finger on her chin, stared up at the ceiling, and breathed in deeply through her nose while she thought. "I guess knowing he'll never hit the same milestones as the rest of you kids," she said. "He'll never get a driver's license, he'll never graduate from high school, and he'll never get married and have children. Things like that are the hardest."

Nothing about how her life had changed — her focus remained on what Berkeley would miss.

I studied the side of Mom's face as she had already turned back to Berkeley and his basketball game. She had evidently already grappled with any disappointments about her own life and felt at peace with her role. Berkeley's future remained her only concern.

For me, a new unrest was developing. For the first time I considered the things Berkeley could not have.

Perhaps I had not paid attention to Berkeley's dreams in the past, but now I began to hear them.

"A party at my blue house," he told me one day.

"You want to have a blue house and have a party?" I asked him.

"Yes, hamburgers."

"Mmm, that sounds good; that sounds like a fun party," I told him.

"Yellow dog?" He looked at me hopefully, and I tried to imagine Berk hosting a party in a blue house, everyone eating hamburgers and a yellow lab running around, getting in the way.

With Berkeley, every dream had a color assigned to it. He wanted a blue house, a yellow dog, and a green truck. And oh, how he wanted a green truck. He began to point them out to me on the street and talk about driving his own green truck.

My heart began to ache a little with what I suspect Mom had felt for years. The yellow dog, I could see that happening — but the blue house, out of the question. So many of his dreams could never come true.

But for some reason, even though completely unreasonable, I wanted him to have the green truck. This one thing I wanted more than all the others. Perhaps it was because Mom had specifically said, "He'll never get a driver's license" that I wanted it so badly.

I began to hatch an idea, and a few days later I stood in the dusty driveway, nervously shifting my weight from one foot to the other while Leigh gave his pickup a tune-up. "I think I could teach Berk to drive on that old race track you guys made," I said addressing his backside. To call the rutted path around our eight acres a racetrack was a stretch. Ethan and Leigh had sped an old rundown car around the perimeter of the place until a distinguishable course had slowly materialized, but it resembled more of a path than a road.

Leigh emerged from under the hood and gave me a puzzled look. "Why do you want to teach Berk to drive?" he asked. "He's only 14."

"I don't know. I guess, I think it'd be kind of fun." I replied. "He doesn't get to do all the things us other kids get to do, and he really wants a truck. I just think it would be good for him."

"Hmph," he replied.

"It's not like I think he could drive on regular roads or anything. It'd give him a sense of accomplishment, and you were driving by the time you were eight," I argued. I felt my confidence waver as Leigh stuck his head back under the hood.

Over the next couple of weeks, I tried gaining support from other members of the family; but their responses, much like Leigh's reaction, did not give me a lot of hope. They listened to me talk and then said nothing, and I convinced myself that they thought it was an idiotic idea.

I knew the plan sounded crazy, but I also knew how handy Berkeley had become. Given time and patience, I believed he could learn to drive under supervision. Then one evening I heard the clanging as a vehicle crossed the metal bridge at the end of our driveway. The sound of clattering and rattling continued up the drive, and I went to investigate. Looking out the living room window, I saw Leigh towing an ancient pick-up truck, a green Datsun which sported several dents and a few spots of rust.

I could feel my forehead crinkling into a question mark as I stepped onto the front porch and leaned across the railing.

Leigh climbed out of the truck, glanced up at me, and said, "I was telling my co-worker, Scott, about you wanting to teach Berkeley to drive. He gave me the truck."

Excitement exploded in me. Leigh had understood. He wanted this for Berkeley too. I wasn't crazy! We could do this.

"Berkeley, Berkeley!" I yelled. "Berkeley, come look." Eagerly I rushed to inspect the truck.

Berkeley came around the back side of the garage as I kept yelling for him to "come look."

"See what Leigh got for you. It's your own green truck, Berkeley."

I pulled the driver's door open and then froze.

"Are you kidding me? It's a stick shift! Berkeley needs an automatic. How are we going to teach him to drive a manual?"

Leigh returned my accusing look as if he had prepared himself for this confrontation.

"Hey, it was free. If he's capable of learning to drive, he can learn to drive a manual."

For the first time, a little niggling of doubt crept into the back of my mind. *I can barely drive a stick,* I thought to myself. *How on earth am I going to teach Berk to drive one?* And then I realized just how badly I wanted this to be a success. I decided not to let this obstacle stand in my way. We, no, Berkeley had a truck now, and I would go to whatever lengths necessary to make it work.

"How do you like your truck, Berkeley?" Ethan asked.

"Green truck!" Berkeley nodded with enthusiasm.

"Think you can drive it?" asked Dad.

Berkeley fiddled with the latch on the hood, and Leigh helped him lift it and pointed out the battery and the engine.

I had not anticipated getting the family on board this quickly, but I knew we needed to have one more discussion.

"Maybe, for consistency's sake, only one of us should be Berkeley's teacher." I knew I wanted it to be me, but I had to tread carefully here. "You know how Berkeley is when someone crabs at him?"

"Yeah," Mom agreed. "You can't yell at him or he won't want to drive anymore."

Everyone stood around looking at the ground or the sky while considering Berkeley's aggravating habit of repeating the same mistake over and over. You might explain, reason, and reduce yourself to begging him to stop. Sometimes the breakthrough came quickly; most of the time it did not. Not grouching at him took colossal patience and resolve. At the same time, teaching him to drive would be so thrilling.

I nervously twisted a strand of my hair. Leigh had secured the vehicle; so, to be fair, maybe he should be the one to teach him.

"It'd better be Laura," Amy said. "She's the only one who won't end up yelling at him."

I sensed disappointment from Leigh, but slowly he nodded his head in agreement.

"Once he knows how to drive, of course everyone else can drive with him," I said. "It's just while he's learning."

Leigh grinned and threw the keys to me. I climbed into the driver's seat, and with Leigh beside me took a few spins around the place just to get a feel for the clutch and the shifting. I lurched and jerked around the property in that ancient vehicle and wondered how I could successfully teach a 14-year-old boy with Down syndrome to drive when I could barely keep the truck from dying every time I started.

I figured clutching, braking, shifting, and pressing the gas pedal were going to be the biggest challenges but decided they could not be split into separate lessons since they happen almost simultaneously. He would have to learn how to start smoothly, and I would help him shift no matter how many tries it took before he learned the art of pushing and releasing clutch, brake, and gas pedals.

During the first lesson, I showed him the mechanics of pushing in the clutch and releasing it. "Push in this pedal with your foot, Berk. No, no the other foot," I told him pointing to the clutch and patting his left leg. "Good...good job. Now," and here I placed my hand over his, "shift it down and over. Good job!" I kept the encouragement coming. "Lift your foot up slowly, and push this peddle with your other foot."

The engine roared; we lurched forward — the truck died. After a few more times of practice, he began to understand the motion of releasing the clutch and pushing the gas. Now the engine just raced, and although we would still pitch forward in an alarming fashion, he didn't kill it every single time. Before the end of that first lesson, Berkeley could push in the clutch, shift into first, release the clutch, and press the gas pedal on his own.

I showed him how to push the brake with his right foot. Every time I said, "Push in the brake, Berkeley," he jammed it down bringing us to an abrupt and jolting stop. Whenever a tree loomed in front of us and I feared we would smash into it, I shortened that to simply shouting "Brake." After a few lessons, he reached a fair level of consistency in clutching, shifting, and stopping. The only element we had not tackled was steering, in comparison a relatively easy component of driving. But, for some reason the concept of turning the wheel in the direction he wanted to go seemed as foreign to him as another language. As we bumped around the track in first gear, I frantically yelled and gestured "Go that way, go that way, Berkeley." Finally, to keep us from colliding with yet another grove of trees, I shrieked "Brake!" and he obediently slammed on the brakes killing the engine. After a minute, he started the truck, released the clutch, shifted into reverse, and backed away from the trees. Patiently I tried to explain how the steering wheel worked, but moments later I hollered, "brake, Brake, BRAKE!"

Since I never let him take the truck out of first, we experienced minimal damage even though we rarely had a lesson where we did not run over a pile of brush, into a tree, or end up wedged between two logs. Each time we got stuck, I got out and pushed while Berk shifted into reverse and pressed the gas pedal.

Heaps of brush drew him with magnetic force. One day, while I energetically shouted "Turn the wheel! Berkeley, turn the wheel that way," he ran us right on top of a big pile of branches Mom had pushed together with the tractor. As we stood surveying the situation together, he gave out a big sigh and said, "Dad be mad." The daily driving lesson ended when Berk and I could not get the truck unstuck by ourselves.

I took his hand and went in search of Dad. We found him in the shop, and Berkeley gave him an apologetic look and said, "Stuck Dad."

"What?" Dad said in mock agitation. "Again?" but he smiled, and Berkeley knew Dad wasn't angry at all, just teasing.

Then one day, the steering clicked with him. And as we rattled along as fast as that little truck could go in first gear, I almost relaxed over on my side of the bench seat. Whenever we encountered a downward slope, we picked up decent momentum. And then we came to our favorite spot where the road dipped down and then back up on a curve. On the left of the now well-established race path, a deep creek flowed slowly across the south end of the property, and to our right a stand of maple trees fenced us in. The fit was tight, and I did not want to deviate off the track.

"Not too fast," I told him. But Berkeley, with newfound confidence, gunned the engine. Before I could react, we careened down — straight toward the creek. I imagined us bobbing in the middle of the water before slowly sinking, and it occurred to me that Dad might very possibly be mad this time. Instead, we curved upward and now faced the trees. Berkeley took this opportune time to take his eyes off the path, look me straight in the eyes, and yell, "Hang on, HONEY!"

White knuckled, my left hand clutched the dashboard and my right hand the widow frame. The literal thudding of my heart filled my ears, and yet I felt a thrill zinging through my body. When we came into the clearing and Berkeley eased up on the gas, I looked at him. His face did not resemble that of a handicapped child. It was the face of a proud teenager.

I swallowed hard past the lump growing in my throat and said, "That was fun; let's do it again."

That evening during dinner, I related the "Hang on, Honey" story to the family. "I think he's ready to take you for a ride," I said, nodding at Leigh.

The next afternoon, Leigh and his buddy Tom packed themselves into the tiny cab with Berk, their legs and arms crammed in so tightly they could hardly move. As they took off, I gave them a strict reminder, "Don't be gruff with him."

I could hear the whooping and hollering as I trudged up the back-porch steps.

When the boys came into the house a few minutes later, they had the decided look of ones who had endured a harrowing experience.

"Did you never teach Berkeley what stop meant?" Leigh asked.

"Of course, I did."

"Well, I don't think you actually used the word, 'Stop.'" he said. "Berk was kind of showing off for us and lost his focus. He was headed straight for some trees, but we remembered you telling us not to yell at him; so, we said, 'Stop, Berkeley, stop.' But he just kept going straight towards those trees. We were packed in there like sardines; so, we couldn't move our arms to the steering wheel or get our legs over to the brake. We started yelling 'Stop, Berkeley STOP!' But he didn't stop. We were ready to hit the trees and Tom yelled 'Put on the BRAKE!' When Berkeley heard the word brake, he hit it so hard we almost flew through the windshield."

"Hmmm," I said and then started laughing. "Come to think of it, I did always say 'Push on the brake, Berkeley." I had never changed my phraseology — only shortened it to the word, "brake."

What a fun summer we had! As silly as it might sound, taking rides with Berkeley in the old green truck grew into an event. Friends and people from church asked Berkeley to take them for rides. If we hosted a dinner or threw a barbeque, our friends asked, "When's Berk going to take us out in his truck?"

When the time came, Berkeley went over to the truck, lifted the hood and ceremoniously adjusted things while all the friends jumped into the bed of the truck. Sometimes as many as 12 people climbed aboard. I still sat in the cab with Berkeley to supervise. Occasionally, he got carried away with all the attention and needed a little reminder to "Go that way" or to "Put on the brake."

Berkeley shifted into first, and the passengers in the back started cheering and laughing. The highlight of every ride came when we dipped down by the creek. As Berkeley hit the accelerator, he yelled every single time, "Hang on, Honey!" And Mom heard the screaming passengers in her kitchen.

We used that truck for several years to bring in wood from the back pasture or to pick a load of rocks out of the field. We always let Berkeley drive it out and back. After all, it was his truck. One day it refused to start and no amount of fiddling around under the hood made a difference. The green Datsun had a long life and happy sunset years fulfilling one of Berkeley's dreams.

I wondered if Berkeley would ask for another truck, but he did not seem to miss driving. He had met his aspiration of owning and driving a truck, and he moved on to other ambitions.

Driving lessons took place many years ago, but the other day, I took a corner a little too quickly and yelled to myself, "Hang on, Honey!"

HELP SECTION

Being overly protective is a huge temptation, but we all grow when we fulfill our dreams and goals. Although getting Berkeley a driver's license was completely out of the question, we found a unique solution to help him reach a personal goal.

Chapter 13
Berkeley at School

After numerous attempts to focus on the spreadsheet in front of me, I gave up and put all my effort into prayer. Audible words never passed through my lips, but the thoughts in my heart called out loudly. "God, please keep our Berkeley safe. Please, please don't let anyone hurt him today." My prayers, basic and uncreative, were nonetheless deep with emotion.

My throat ached with unshed tears. Nervously I fiddled with a pencil. Holding it loosely between middle and index finger, I tapped it repeatedly with my thumb in a subconscious act of distraction.

The entire family felt powerless that day. Dad working on huge pieces of machinery, Mom distracting herself in the garden, Ethan and Leigh at their jobs, and Amy in her college classes — all of us wondering how Berkeley was doing and sending out silent prayers for God to guard our little boy during his first day of junior high.

When Berkeley started elementary school, we felt mild nervousness but also had confidence in the guilelessness of children and believed he would not be bullied. And the minor fears we harbored had dissipated quickly when Berkeley's first grade teacher made a video of her special education class and took it to the class-rooms of the typically developing children.

"These are boys and girls who want to have friends just like you," she told them. "Remember to be kind and to talk to them."

Wisely, she prepared the way, and the first six years of his happy education flew by. He learned to read simple words, solve math problems with piles of plastic spoons, and print his name even though every "e" had a way of persistently turning out backwards. He decorated our house generously with wobbly clay vases and plaster handprints.

Turning Berkeley over to the protection of an elementary school teacher had made us anxious, but we dreaded the first day of junior high. Elementary kids maintain a fair amount of compassion, but I worried about a change that occurs in middle school. Too often the desire to fit in with the cool kids, regardless of the cost to their conscience and morality, drives teens to do things they later in life wish they had not done. And that scared me. As these kids tried to fit in, would Berkeley become the brunt of their jokes, their taunting, and maybe even worse?

But Berkeley came home from his first day of junior high happy. He came home his second day, and third

– no scrapes or bruises – smiling and confident. After a few weeks, we stopped worrying. If anything, Berkeley seemed even happier in junior high than grade school.

Berkeley continued to improve his reading and math skills; but instead of crafts, he now attended classes with the purpose of improving his life and social skills.

Twice a week Berkeley boarded a school bus and traveled over to the high school for Home Economics. As he walked through the doors, students descended upon him, and a class of mostly girls showered him with attention. They hugged him and tied an apron around his waist. The girls campaigned relentlessly to have Berkeley on "their team," and the teacher set a fair rotation so that everyone could experience a little Berkeley. The teacher had no other complaints and welcomed the spark of fun Berkeley brought to class.

Back at junior high school, Berkeley's popularity swelled to new heights as he started making and serving no-bake cookies in the cafeteria. Soon there wasn't a kid in the school who didn't know Berkeley. Instead of being the butt of jokes, Berkeley settled into the cool crowd. So much so that the school administration felt safe incorporating Berkeley into more mainstream classes and that landed him in a body building physical education class.

At first, lifting weights seemed innocuous enough, but one day Berkeley walked up behind Amy, wrapped his arms around her waist, and picked her up. "Whoa,

Berkeley," she yelled. "Put me down." He set her on the ground and promptly walked over to Mom and picked her up. They both outweighed him by at least 50 pounds.

"How did he get so strong?" Amy asked.

"Oh, they have him lifting weights at school," Mom answered nonchalantly.

"Do you think that's a good idea?" Amy asked with skepticism. "I mean, he's really strong, and don't you think he might hurt somebody without meaning to?"

Then one day I stopped by for a visit and Berkeley lifted me up too. Only he didn't put me down when I asked.

Amy and I nagged Mom until she called the school.

The PE teacher, a fit, middle-aged man, did not see why helping Berkeley build his strength should be a problem.

But Berkeley became stronger and stronger. Some days he hugged the breath right out of my lungs. I watched him lugging logs around outside, and Amy and I begged Mom to call the school again. "This doesn't seem smart Mom. Do you remember reading *Of Mice and Men?* I know he'd never hurt anybody on purpose, but what if he does by accident?"

Mom made another call to the PE teacher, but he convinced her that he knew better. "I think you're being overprotective, Mrs. Smith. We are just helping him build his strength".

Three weeks later Amy answered the ringing phone, and the PE teacher on the other end of the line sheepishly asked to speak to Mom.

"Mrs. Smith, I think you may have a point about that weightlifting thing with Berkeley."

"Oh?"

"Well, the thing is, I was wrestling around with him today, and he got me in a choke hold. I couldn't get away. I could not break free from him. He is," he paused and then continued. "He is very strong. He's so small and all, I don't think anyone would suspect it, but you're right, he could hurt someone by accident."

That ended Berkeley's stint of weightlifting.

Just before school let out for summer break, Berkeley begged me to take him to a football game. He had been talking about the Bears a lot, and I always wanted him to be able to do the things other kids got to do; so, I agreed. After buying popcorn, we made our way into the bleachers where a steady stream of kids stopped by to say "Hi." So many teenagers stopped by our seats that I never did see much of that game.

My anxious prayers at the beginning of the year had been answered in the sweetest way possible. Not only accepted within the school; Berkeley had impacted the lives of these young people in a meaningful way.

Long after Berkeley left his school years behind, I would run into these kids, now adults. They were better people, kind people, forever changed by the investment they had made in Berkeley's life.

HELP SECTION

Like it or not, people are always going to be curious. Berkeley's first-grade teacher, by talking directly to the other children about Berkeley and his classmates, removed any mystery about their condition. In a respectful way, she allowed the children to be inquisitive. In this way they could identify with the need for kindness and friendship; and because of this empathy taught by a caring teacher, they took Berkeley into their circle right from the beginning.

Sometimes we end up trying to make our children exactly like every other child, and in doing so try to hide anything that occurs which might fall outside of what we call "normal." Because that teacher did not try to cover up the differences but helped others embrace Berkeley's circumstances, he became accepted — even loved for exactly who he is.

Staring, pointing, and rude comments will never be okay; but allowing for open dialogue with the people in your life may be the very thing that allows them to have a normal relationship with your child.

Chapter 14
Finding Dad's Letter

I opened the closet door and sighed as I saw the stacked boxes on the floor and top shelf. How long had they sat there without me ever looking in them? Convinced most of the contents would soon be in the garbage or on their way to the thrift store, I pulled them out one at a time and stacked them against the wall. I surveyed the empty closet with the pleasure a clean space always gives me before turning back to the task of sorting through all those old memories.

I powered through the first box of knickknacks — mostly junk I had saved from my youth. Next, I tackled a stack of elementary school papers trying to save only the cutest works of art from my childhood. Feeling proud of my progress, I transferred a third box to the dining room table and cut the yellowed tape holding it closed. On top lay a bundle of carbon copy letters.

Immediately, I knew what they represented. Long before photocopy machines or home computers, Dad used to sit down on a Sunday afternoon and crank a thick stack of paper into his manual typewriter. Between each regular piece of paper, he carefully positioned a piece of black, inky carbon paper.

His mother would receive the top copy because her eyes were the oldest, and then the following copies went to his many siblings scattered throughout the United States. The very last copy went into a file, and now I held those old copies in my hands.

I sank to the floor and pulled the old letters into my lap. What a treasure! Quickly I began scanning through them for news of myself as a little girl. Dad wrote the first letter in the collection about the time I turned six years old, and I found myself smiling as I saw my little self through my Father's eyes. Those old letters captured little snippets of my childhood transporting me back to the summer of 1976 when my sister and I picked cherries from our tree, drooling over the pie we knew Mom would make. In the next letter, Dad recorded how Amy and I gobbled handfuls of parsley from the garden before he could rototill over it.

Flipping to the back of the stack, I came to a few written in 1978, the last letters of the file. I closed my eyes while I remembered those long-ago days and realized that since Berkeley was born in September of 1978, Dad had likely run out of time to write after he was born.

I thumbed through those final letters and came across a unique one — addressed to my aunts and uncles – not my grandma. Dated October 1, 1978, Dad would have written this letter two and a half weeks after Berkeley's birth. An unexpected chill caused me to scoot over on the floor into the warmth of a sunbeam, and I began to read:

> One thing which we hadn't told a lot of people up to now, mainly because we didn't know for sure and were waiting for the return of certain tests to verify early diagnosis, is the fact that Berkeley has Down syndrome. We were over to see him this past Wednesday, and the reports had returned; and it is confirmed that he does have Down syndrome, which is a genetic abnormality, and means quite simply, that he will be mentally slow. We don't know at this time how severe it will be….

The page blurred in front of me, and I realized Dad must have called Grandma but didn't have the energy to call each of his siblings and explain it to them in person. I blinked the tears away and kept reading.

> He's a cute baby, and we love him and want him home awfully badly. It was a shocking blow when we were first informed of the possibility, especially as the initial possibility was told to us at 3:30 in the morning one day after he was born; but time and prayer make a difference, and by the time it was confirmed, we were quite ready to accept it. Not something we would have chosen for ourselves, but as long as God felt that this

was what we needed, we are ready to do our best
in raising him.

It's really unfair for me to give this news
to you in a letter, because to say that we have
a son that will be mentally disabled, in itself,
sounds so bleak and discouraging. One tends
to project oneself 15 or 20 years into the future
and see a handicapped child that is a stranger
to you. When we realize, however, that it will
be a matter of daily loving him and taking care
of him, and watching him grow, and growing
to love him more as he grows, it's not such a
fearsome thing. Anyway, we thank God for him,
and are super anxious to get him home.

I laid the letter onto the neat stack of its companions
and wrapped my arms around myself. Late sunshine
shone through the west window and warmed me and the
letters as I sat on the floor gently rocking back and forth.
Tears ran unchecked into my lap. We had just celebrated
Berkeley's 18th birthday. We had entered those 15 to
20 years of the future Dad had mentioned in his letter.

I picked up the letters and returned them to the
box. Standing, I went to the kitchen where I had a
picture of Berkeley stuck to the refrigerator. Once again,
I closed my eyes as my mind reached back through the
years. In my memory's eye, I could see Dad standing
in the living room when he told us other kids about
Berkeley having Down syndrome and his struggle to
explain what it meant.

That letter gave me a tiny glimpse into how my parents had felt. They had been fearful of the unknown and too exhausted to keep having the conversation over and over with loved ones. Instead, Dad had written a letter in which he hinted at the guilt he felt for not telling them in person.

During those stressful, unknown days, Dad had seen into the future, and he had been right. Berkeley was our gift from God. We had loved him more with every passing day; and now, we could not, would not, imagine life without him.

As we hung on through those eight weeks of hospitalization, hoping we could bring him home one day, we all fell in love with a fragile little baby. I remembered holding Berkeley for the first time and knowing that I would love him forever.

Berkeley had been the perfect gift for our family.

HELP SECTION

Parents

Finding out that your child has a disability brings with it overwhelming emotions. Finding enough strength to deal with your own questions and feelings may leave you paralyzed. This is a time for you to take care of yourself. You may not have the strength to explain it over and over and field questions, and that is okay.

Sending a letter or asking someone else to tell your best friend may seem "unfair," but it may preserve some much-needed strength. Retelling and dealing with the condolences in those first days may prove to be too much. You will have many chances to talk to your friends and loved ones in the weeks, months, and years to come.

It is okay to let someone else break the news or send a letter.

Friends/Acquaintances

You may consider yourself the BEST friend and feel hurt that you heard the news by someone other than the parents. But many people find that it is easier to tell a stranger difficult news than it is to tell a loved one. Strangers' feelings don't matter, but a best friend's do. You as the dear friend will hurt alongside of them, and they may instinctively know they cannot handle your emotions in addition to their own. You will have your chance to listen and hand over tissues. Put your hurt feelings aside and be ready to hug your friend the next time you meet.

Chapter 15

The Mop

"I can't figure out what's happened to my mop," Mom said. "I'm sure I put it out on the back porch to dry last Saturday. I don't remember bringing it back in, but where could it have gotten itself to?"

"Did it fall off the porch?" I asked.

"I looked all around the porch, even under it," Mom said with frustration edging her voice.

"What about the basement? Did you maybe put it in the basement?"

"Why would I take it into the basement?" Mom's voice conveyed an ever so slight annoyance at my stupid question. "I just can't imagine where it is."

We did not have to wonder much longer. That afternoon Dad rounded the corner of the garage and noticed the mop handle standing against an old stack of lumber. His eyes traveled down the length of the handle where the charred remains of the mop head ended in a bucket of water.

He pulled the mop out and stared at it. "What in the world?" he mumbled. Stooping down, he picked up the bucket and went to find Berkeley.

Behind the pump house, Berkeley was busy at his wood pile. As Dad rounded the corner, Berkeley's little, but tough muscled arms lifted the splitting maul and dropped it heavily onto the end of an upright log cracking it in two. He leaned down and picked up one of the halves and set it in place for the second splitting. Looking up he smiled at Dad and then seeing the mop and bucket, his expression changed to obvious distress.

"Sorry, Dad! Very bad. Very bad! So sorry, Dad."

"What happened?" Dad asked sternly.

"So naughty, sorry Dad. Scare you" (which really meant, *I did something that scared me very badly, and I'm very, very sorry).*

Dad stood there looking at Berkeley and trying to piece together in his mind what had taken place.

"I show you Dad." Berkeley said as he started toward the garage. Inside Berkeley found the lighter for the welder and flicked it on as he motioned toward the mop.

"Sorry, Dad! Not do again. Very naughty!"

We will never know exactly what transpired, but we believe Berkeley developed a curiosity for fire, and it held a certain fascination for him. One Saturday afternoon a perfectly good thing to burn presented itself in the form of Mom's mop, nice and dry from sitting in the hot sunshine. Having seen Dad use the lighter to start the welder, it all seemed harmless enough until he held a flaming torch. The more he swished it around in the air, the larger the flames grew.

From his reaction, admission of sorrow, and repeated, "Scare you," we know with confidence that he experienced some fearful moments before he thought of dousing it in a bucket of water. We don't know how he knew what to do in the case of "fire gone wild;" but thankfully, he figured it out.

The mop burning incident left us all a little shaken. The whole thing could have ended horribly.

Those periods of parenting were hard for my parents. Dad stood looking at his son, this little man who still had the mind of a child — so many grown-up things that Berkeley would never get to do. Something as simple as lighting a fire — and it had nearly ended in disaster. Dad did not want to punish Berkeley, but he had to make sure Berkeley never played with fire again.

"No fire without Dad!" he finally told Berkeley.

"No Dad. Not want to do." Berkeley responded. "So bad!" Berkeley put his arms around Dad's waist, and Dad hugged him back. Dad did not doubt that Berkeley would give fire a wide berth in the future.

HELP SECTION

Children with disabilities want to experience life. They absorb more than we realize, but they cannot always articulate what they think.

Try to treat them as you would your other children. If you have a campfire, let them help you lay out the kindling and wood. Show them how to light the fire; and if they are capable, let them have a turn while you supervise. The more you involve them, the less likely they will want to experiment on their own. Use the experience to talk about the dangers of fire. Show them how things burn up in the fire and how to stay back so they don't get burned. Don't frighten them but let them see that the fire is hot and could hurt them. This is what you would do with your other children because you expect they will one day be lighting their own fires. Try to realize how much your child with a disability feels left out when you don't teach them these life skills too.

Let them help you pump gas, push the lawn mower, or paint a fence. Berkeley loves to bake cookies. Even though he doesn't read well, I show him the recipe and bit by bit he is learning what 1 cup means. Once I have helped him mix the ingredients, I'm done. All I need to do is help him put the cookies in and out of the oven. He does the rest of the work.

As much as you may want to bubble wrap your child, you cannot; so look for all kinds of life's teachable opportunities.

Chapter 16
Graduation

Mom waited for a lull in the laughter and storytelling. Our family, as we often did on Sundays, had come from our various homes to Mom and Dad's house for dinner. We had added a sister-in-law, Loretta, Leigh's wife, to our family; and Berkeley adored her.

"We need to talk about Berkeley and graduation." Conversations ceased as we turned our attention to Mom. "Berkeley brought a note home from school saying he could walk with the graduating class, but instead of giving him a diploma, they would give him a certificate of completion."

"He's done with school then?" Amy asked.

"Yes, he's only allowed to stay in public school through the age of 21; so this is it."

"Um, so it'd look like he was being given a diploma?" I asked. "But really it would just be a certificate saying he attended school."

"Something like that. What do you kids think?"

What did we think? We remembered a kid in our own school who had never applied himself, never had to do the work for a diploma, but the school passed him from grade to grade until one day he stood on the platform and accepted the diploma placed in his hands. It had smacked of unfairness to us, and even though Berkeley's situation was different, Ethan said what we all feared.

"I think the kids who studied, did homework, and wrote papers to earn a diploma might resent having it look like Berkeley's getting one too."

"They might, and that wouldn't be good for Berkeley." Leigh added.

A quiet sadness settled over us, and Berkeley oblivious to the meaning of our words but feeling the shift in moods sighed loudly and said, "Oh no!"

How many times had we made these decisions? Shielding Berkeley from resentment he could not comprehend. We so wanted Berkeley to have everything other kids had, but as a family we needed to consider the big picture. We wanted to pave the way for his acceptance by others. Putting him in a position where hard feelings could develop might undo years of careful planning.

"If we don't tell him, he might not know what he's missing," I offered.

We stared at each other in glum silence already knowing what Mom would tell the school.

Later I helped Mom compose the note we sent to the school letting them know Berkeley would not walk, and I remembered her words to me years earlier. "The hardest thing is that he won't hit milestones like you other kids. He'll never get a driver's license, and he'll never graduate from high school."

An ache in my heart made me wish graduation would hurry up and be over.

The following Friday, we invaded our parents' house, once again eating free food, teasing each other, and retelling stories of our not-so-distant past glory days.

"I almost called you earlier this week because I got a call from Berkeley's class counselor." Mom our "Steady Eddie," not often given to emotional demonstrations either jubilant or dispirited, was the sort of person whose attitude calmly said, *Here are the facts, now what will you do with them?* But today, her disposition sparkled. "You're not going to believe what he said. He told me the kids in Berkeley's class are upset because we won't allow Berkeley to walk in graduation. They said, 'Berkeley's been a part of us since we started first grade. Can his parents be so mean that they won't let him walk with us? We won't feel like we've graduated if Berkeley isn't there.'"

We looked at Mom with incredulous eyes. If those kids only knew how agonizing that decision had been for us.

Because Berkeley didn't start school until he was a little older, he had "advanced" through the grades with mostly the same students year after year. The kids he would walk with were the same ones he had played with during recess in first grade.

"He's going to look so cute in a cap and gown," Loretta said. "Do we need to order them?"

"I already did," Mom told us.

"Do they make them small enough for him?" I asked.

"Yes, they do, and I made sure they knew he's only 4' 10" tall.

Instead of dreading graduation day, I now anticipated it with a lightheartedness as strong as the sadness I had felt one week earlier.

On graduation day, we drove across town to the Bellevue Community College gymnasium because the Tahoma High School did not have facilities large enough to accommodate the large graduating class and their families.

Climbing half-way up the bleachers, we found an open space large enough for our entire family and took our seats on the hard aluminum benches.

"Tell me why we thought this was so important?" Leigh asked as we braced ourselves for the long ceremony to come.

"His teacher called yesterday to let us know he'll walk in with the tallest kid in the graduating class so we can spot him when he walks in," Mom informed us.

When at last *Pomp and Circumstance* began to play, we searched the throng of royal blue caps and gowns for Berkeley. And then a kid, head and shoulders above everyone else walked into the gym with Berkeley beside him. I looked at them, the tall teen for signs of resentment and Berkeley for any traces of fear. I saw neither in those heads held high as they coolly sauntered to their seats.

Berkeley sat on the edge of the basketball court, and we began the long wait for those 20 seconds of the two hours that mattered — the moment when the man standing on the stage read his name and handed him a certificate.

I fanned myself in the stifling hot gymnasium, and Berkeley took off his cap. His teacher walked over and encouraged him to put it back on his head, but Berkeley promptly removed it and mopped the sweat on his forehead. I made my way down to the floor and quietly tried to reason with him about the cap. He ignored me.

I climbed back to my spot on the bleachers and tried to figure the math on how long it would take to read through the over 300 names and distribute the accompanying diplomas. My back ached, and the voice below had only struggled through the names beginning with H.

With the announcement of each name, I noticed a small pod of friends and family stood and cheered from various areas of the bleachers. Knowing the reserved nature of my family, I stage whispered down the row to them, "When Berkeley's name is called, we have to stand and cheer."

They looked at me as if I had grown a third eye and shook their heads as if to say, *Uh, no, polite clapping will be sufficient.*

Hoping the people behind me did not mind my ongoing dialogue, I employed my strategy of guilt. "Do you want him to be the ONLY one who has no one cheering for him? He needs to hear us cheering for him or he might think he did something wrong."

Well, no, they didn't want that; so with reluctance, they agreed to stand and cheer when his time came.

As we neared the end of the R names, someone prompted Berkeley to stand and walk to the edge of the stage. His special education teacher stuffed the cap back onto his head, and Berkeley walked proudly to the platform, cap in place.

We scooched to the edge of the hard bleachers, ready to stand, clap, and yell for our Berkeley. And then they called his name, Berkeley Glen Smith. The gymnasium erupted. On the floor, the entire graduating class rose as one person and began to cheer. Behind the students, the faculty stood, wide smiles on their faces as they put their hands together to applaud my brother. All around us and across the gym, friends and families from the other students stood, clapped, and cheered.

My legs had suddenly become weak, and I could not seem to force sound past the lump in my throat. I finally managed to stand and put my hands together, but still no sound would come. I smiled, but I could feel tears trickling down my cheeks. Where did those tears come from? I looked down the row at my family and saw the looks of disbelief on their faces; and then suddenly we all started smiling, laughing, clapping, and hugging each other. The interruption probably lasted less than 30 seconds, but the restless mood had changed to one of electricity. The rest of the ceremony passed in a blur. I often wondered if the students had planned this. I think they had. They stood so quickly, and to have their families stand as well? It had not been a halfhearted attempt to honor him. This group of young people loved my brother and determined to make his day special.

That action of acceptance and love burned into my mind and heart forever. I watched as Berkeley accepted his certificate of completion and walked back to his seat. He took off the cap and wiped his forehead.

After graduation, we waited for a long time while students hugged Berkeley and kissed him goodbye.

Most of those students went off to university while Berkeley worked at a job recycling cardboard. They would likely never see Berkeley again, but I believe they took a little Berkeley with them.

Berkeley then and still can barely write his name. The Es always end up backwards, and the letters wander along on the page in large and different sizes. When he introduces himself to a new person, they struggle to understand him. Yet, with his limited communication skills, he had already impacted thousands of lives in a profound way. His disability had allowed several hundred students to learn about compassion and the joy of giving a good gift to someone. They had given Berkeley the gift of a beautiful graduation.

HELP SECTION

Parents

Be willing to accept input from outside your immediate circle. Sometimes your perceptions are skewed because you may be overthinking or worrying too much about the situation. Clearly, we had missed the mark in thinking Berkeley's classmates would not want him there.

Friends/Acquaintances

The gift of inclusion is the greatest contribution you may be able to give a family.

My heart broke over and over as I saw how much Berkeley loved babies and yet for many years was shooed away from infants. In recent years, loving church family has allowed Berkeley supervised opportunities to hold babies.

Others have welcomed him into their Sunday School classes and made him an important part of the group much like his classmates did those years ago during graduation.

Chapter 17

Blinded Eyes

"Laura, can I talk to you for a minute?"

I looked up with surprise at the sound of my supervisor's voice and tried to interpret what it meant. She didn't look angry, and yet an edge to her voice told me something had upset her.

"Sure," I said with more confidence than I felt.

I followed Kim into a private conference room where she said in a hushed voice, "It's about Andrea."

Andrea, our receptionist, had told us with delight a few weeks earlier that after a ten-year gap and at the age of 36, she would add another child to their family. She had laughed telling us she would have teenagers and a toddler in the house at the same time.

I nodded my head and waited for Kim to continue.

"Andrea called me a few minutes ago, and she was very distraught. She'd gone in for some routine tests on her pregnancy, and the doctor told her the initial testing shows she might be carrying a Down syndrome baby." Subconsciously, Kim straightened the maroon chairs around the conference table before continuing. "I don't know what to say to her, Laura. But I'm thinking with your brother and all, you might be a good one to talk to her. You'll know what to say."

I went back to my office and spent several minutes trying to figure out what one did say in situations like this. I sat there at my desk and tried to imagine I was Andrea. What would I want to hear if I were facing her situation?

The more I tried to think of what to say, the more I realized how our situations differed. When my parents told me Berkeley had Down syndrome, I listened and understood with the ears of a little girl and as a sister. But Andrea — she heard these words, "Your child may have Down syndrome." As a mother and a grown woman, she would more fully understand the long-term implications. By the time I understood the magnitude of what it meant to have a child with a disability, I had already lived with Berkeley for many years and could not imagine life without him.

I closed my eyes and prayed for wisdom. *It will be a shock*, I acknowledged to myself. *This isn't what she is expecting*, God seemed to remind me. *She's not even going to know what to think.* Andrea often spoke about being a Christian; so I imagined, after she wrestled with the news for a few days, she would be okay. I finally decided I would simply tell Andrea I was available to talk with her anytime.

The following day I saw her walking toward me down a narrow hallway in our office building. She paused as we met, and I laid my hand on her arm. "Kim told me about your baby. If you want to talk, know that I am here for you." The words seemed a little awkward to me, but with an intensity that surprised me, she took hold of my hand. Her eyes were full of something I didn't understand, but I understood her words.

"Laura, I don't know what to do. They aren't positive the baby has Down syndrome, but I only have two weeks to have an abortion before I can no longer legally abort him."

As an image of Berkeley passed through my consciousness, numb speechlessness took possession of me. Not remembering why I held papers in my hand or where my original destination lay, I pulled my arm out of her grip and walked dazedly back to my office. With the door firmly closed, I laid my head on the desk and sobbed. I saw, or thought I saw, how the rest of the world viewed my brother, and it broke my heart.

Over the next few days, I avoided leaving my office for fear of seeing Andrea. Then toward the end of the week, the entire staff vacated the office for a conference, leaving only Andrea, myself, and the boss with whom we had very little interaction. Normally, I would have attended the conference where most of my co-workers had gone, but this year I had volunteered to be the one to stay back and hold down the fort. I wished I had gone.

Making the situation worse, my supervisor asked
me to work in the front office with Andrea for the next
two days so that she wouldn't have to face the public
alone. In the seven years I worked in that office, I never
saw the office so barren. *God what are you thinking?*
Why do I have to work next to this person who sees
no worth in my brother?

On day one, I spoke civilly to Andrea when necessary
but not otherwise. I felt justified in my anger. On day
two, I began to feel uncomfortable, not sick uncomfortable — but more the feeling you get when you see your
own imperfections the way God sees them.

I sensed God whispering in my ear. *You think you*
are so perfect, Laura. Have you even tried to under-
stand how she is feeling?

Oh yes, God, I understand perfectly well. She is
going to kill her baby.

At lunchtime I did not want to eat, and by 2:30 in
the afternoon, I felt full-on conviction. No matter how
I tried to justify my anger, God reminded me of the
mercy He had extended to me. From somewhere, a verse
from Psalms kept ringing through my head, "If you,
LORD, kept a record of sins, LORD, who could stand?"

I tried to quiet God's voice, but as the day stretched
on, it kept coming back to me and with more strength
each time. I did not understand because I felt justified
in my position.

Due to fly to the Midwest for a week of vacation the next morning, I knew Andrea would either have gone through with the abortion or would have committed to having the baby by the time I returned.

As I straightened my desk, my head throbbed with weariness and my heart ached, but I knew I should not leave her in anger. I stood and leaned over the cubicle wall. "Andrea," my voice sounded unsteady. She looked up at me with sad eyes, and those eyes pierced my heart. Why had I not noticed the sadness earlier?

"Andrea," I began again; and the words that came out of my mouth surprised me. "I'm praying for you." As I said the words, a warmth flowed through my heart, and I cried out to God on her behalf. "Remember this," I told her. "God would never give you something you can't handle. If He decides to give you a baby with Down syndrome, He will give you the grace to deal with a baby with Down syndrome."

That's all I said. She didn't respond, and I left on vacation with a heaviness that weighed me down. I prayed almost constantly that she would not have an abortion.

I returned from my vacation but did not have the heart to ask anyone if Andrea had aborted her child.

Two weeks later, Andrea came to my office door. "Can I come in?" she asked.

I nodded, not trusting myself to speak. As she shut the door behind her, I pulled a chair close to mine.

She sat in the chair I offered and stared at me for several seconds before beginning, "Laura," she whispered, "I want to thank you for what you told me about my baby. I was so confused. I just didn't know what to do." A tear rolled down her cheek, but her voice gathered strength as she continued. "The doctor told me and my husband that the birth of a Down syndrome baby almost always tears a family apart. He told us that our marriage wouldn't survive and for the sake of our other children, we should abort the baby. I didn't want to do that." Another tear chased the first one, and I handed her a tissue.

"But I was SO scared, Laura. When you told me that God wouldn't give us a baby we couldn't handle, I went home and told my husband what you said. And that evening we decided we would not abort this baby no matter what."

And there we sat, two women weeping together, and God whispering into my heart, *Aren't you glad you listened to Me and did it my way?*

That incident was one of the most humbling of my life. I have thanked God many times for not allowing me to speak harshly to her or to judge her outwardly (although I did inwardly). Like so many women, the world had told her a lie at her most vulnerable time and preyed on her fear and confusion. How God managed to use me remains a mystery to me, but He did. I know now, if I had responded with the anger I held in my heart, my words would likely have fallen on deaf ears.

Months later, my friend Andrea gave birth to a perfectly healthy, normal, baby boy. The doctor had been wrong.

HELP SECTION

I believe God created each baby with purpose and design and that abortion is against God's command. However, many women feel they have no choice as healthcare workers urge them, at a time when they are most vulnerable, to terminate their pregnancies. What they are being told is simply not true. Andrea was told that her family would be torn apart. Ironically, the opposite often occurs. Many families bond as they rally to work together to give their new baby the best care.

I have been told countless times by friends, relatives, and co-workers, "Your family is amazing. I have never seen a closer family." Far from tearing us apart, Berkeley drew us closer. Often, we put aside our petty differences to work out a problem for Berkeley. He has been our pride and joy, our rallying point, and a true blessing from God.

If God chooses to place a child with disabilities into your life, He most certainly will fill you with love and the ability to care for that child. And yes, this child will change your life. Some of those changes will be hard, but the true joy your child brings will outweigh the difficulties.

Chapter 18

Step Away from the Calendar

"Sunday, Monday, Tuesday, Wednesday…."

I sat in the living room on the old blue sofa and watched Berkeley holding the phone receiver to his ear. His head leaned to one side with his shoulder hunched up to hold it in place.

I heard my sister's voice interrupting him loud and clear from the other end of the telephone line. "Berkeley, step away from the calendar."

Berkeley continued reciting the days of the week…"Thursday, Friday, Saturday…"

"Berkeley, pleeaase, STEP AWAY from the calendar!"

Berkeley stood in the kitchen, and one hand held the wall calendar open to March while the other traced the days as he repeated them to Amy. He had already covered the weeks of January and February stopping only to comment on birthdays, special occasions, and holidays. Experience told me he would finish all 12 months if someone did not intervene.

In short, Berkeley LOVES calendars; and every New Year, he takes the calendar he received for Christmas and studies it meticulously memorizing all the special days.

He especially loves to go through the calendar with unsuspecting callers. If you get caught on the phone with him in January or February, the experience is downright torturous. For this reason, my parents, long ago, began encouraging him to answer the land line. Most telemarketers do not make it through the first week.

I propped a page from Berkeley's calendar in front of me, July 2008. In his oversized, crooked writing, he had printed the word "Work" on every Monday, Wednesday, and Friday. Sometimes he noted occasions that he anticipated with a simple "Yes." The "Yes" could be awarded for any number of things including a sibling coming for dinner.

If for some bizarre reason, you need to know on what day of the week your birthday falls this year, just ask Berkeley, he will tell you. We have never quite understood why he is obsessed with calendars except that it seems to tie in with his need for order and routine.

Berkeley's routines are both a blessing and a frustration. For instance, we never remind him to brush his teeth, make his lunch for work the next day, or to set his alarm clock to get up in the morning.

However, Berkeley does not appreciate having his routine broken. Recently I took him bowling with a group of friends, something he had asked me to do with him for months. We had a blast, but around 6:30 that evening he reminded me that "Walker Texas Ranger" or "Cowboy" as he likes to call it, came on at 8:00 o'clock. He does not like to miss his favorite show.

He has watched every episode at least a dozen times, worrying when the "bad guys" look like they may get away and then jumping from his chair and enthusiastically cheering for Cowboy when he takes them down with his martial arts moves. At 8:00 Berkeley's mental clock tells him that he should be at home, parked in his easy chair with the television on. As the evening wore on and with the passing of every quarter of an hour, the reminders became more frequent. At 7:45 when he realized I did not plan to take him home in time for the show, he did not throw a fit. Instead, he subjected everybody to an hour of muttering things like "Sorry, no Cowboy tonight. Hmm, 8:00 o'clock, no Cowboy tonight. Sorry, maybe next time. Laura, Cowboy tomorrow?"

One of Berkeley's routines is to spend Saturday night at my house. Most weeks this works out fine, but at least once or twice a month, I have an obligation or reason he cannot come to my house. Berkeley has become used to this disappointment and so usually begins telling my parents early Saturday morning, "Sorry, probably not Laura's house tonight?" After about the sixth or seventh time, they have him call me; and when I answer the phone, he says, "Sorry, probably not house tonight?" I then reassure him he can come or tell him "No, it isn't going to work this week." If I tell him he cannot come this week, he says with hopefulness in his voice, "Maybe next Saturday?"

HELP SECTION

Parents

Letting your child or loved one rule your life with an unreasonable schedule may contribute to your own burn-out or even resentment on the part of your other children. However, clinging to a schedule may help them function in this big world of ours. Learn to strike a balance of give and take. Here are some tips to navigate those schedules.

1. Give as much notice as possible when plans and schedules need to change. Grumpiness may ensue, but given a few minutes to process, they will rearrange their mindset and become used to the idea. You do not need to argue but simply restate the change in plans.
2. Be as definite as possible. The word "maybe" creates anxiety. Try to be up front and give their requests a definite yes or no.

Friends/Acquaintances

Many people think Berkeley's routine is cute, but sometimes it wears the family out and other times may create an embarrassing situation. Because of an inability to process change depending upon the emotional maturity of your friend's child – young or old, occasional outbursts may occur. Do your best to put yourself into the family's shoes. Do not assume these result from a lack of parenting or discipline and understand the family often experiences embarrassment and assumes that others judge them.

Chapter 19
I Spy

"Uncle Berkeley is cheating!" Kyle, covered in little boy sweat, stood on the lawn and looked up at me where I stood on the deck.

"Oh, Honey, I don't think he is trying to cheat. He just doesn't understand how to play your version of tag."

"Well, he's cheating, and I think he should sit out for a while."

I bit the bottom of my lip and tried to think of it from Kyle's perspective. I suppose it did seem like Berkeley was cheating so I tried to explain.

"Remember, Kyle. Uncle Berkeley has trouble hearing and also his brain doesn't work like your brain. Sometimes he really doesn't understand. We have to be patient with him."

"He's cheating." Kyle stated with resolution, "And I think he should sit out."

I felt a pang in my heart. I wanted my nephew to understand — to give Berkeley a pass because he really didn't understand the complexities of this hybrid version of tag. Berkeley so much wanted to play with the other kids and feel included.

"Just let him play, Kyle. He doesn't know when he's it or not it; so just let him run around with you."

"It's not fair, and he should sit out."

I had not prepared myself for this, and I thought I could actually feel my heart leaking blood. I knew other kids might not understand Berkeley, but I had assumed my nieces and nephews would automatically understand and sympathize with him.

"Have you guys tried the lawn bowling game we brought over?" I asked hoping to interest Kyle in something else. I did not like this conversation, and I needed to think about it some more.

One day several months and many conversations later, I picked Kyle and Rachael up from my parents' house. They sat in the back seat of my car with Berkeley and happily chatted away at him.

After a few minutes, Kyle reached up and tapped me on the shoulder, "Uncle Berkeley doesn't talk funny. Some people might think he does, but he doesn't. Uncle Berkeley just speaks a different language."

I knew Kyle still struggled to make sense of why and how Berkeley differed from other adults, but oh how I loved his empathetic effort to work it out in his mind.

Then Kyle looked over at Rachael and said, "Let's teach Uncle Berkeley to play I Spy."

"Okay," she said. "Uncle Berkeley, this is how you play."

She delved into a lengthy description of how to play with Kyle interrupting at frequent intervals to offer clarifying statements. When she finished her convoluted account on "how to play," she asked, "Do you understand, Uncle Berkeley?"

Uncle Berkeley responded, as he usually did when someone asked him a question, with a very convincing, "Yes."

I knew Berkeley didn't have the foggiest idea about what Rachael had just explained to him. So, I butted in, "Oh, I'm not sure he really understands. Maybe we should try a different game."

"Oh no, he understands. Don't you Uncle Berkeley? You understand, right?"

"Yes."

"See Auntie Laura. He understands."

"Well..."

"Kyle, you go first and show Uncle Berkeley how to play."

I felt another tag episode coming on and drove in miserable silence while the first round of I Spy commenced between Kyle and Rachael.

When finished, Kyle said, "See Uncle Berkeley, it's easy. Now it's your turn. Do you have something in mind?"

"Yes," Berkeley said.

Knowing he didn't understand the question, I thought quickly. Surely I could pull the wool over two little kids' eyes.

"Is it outside?" I asked making my voice lilt so Berkeley would say, "Yes."

"Yes," he answered.

"Is it blue?" I asked with such a sad tone to my voice that he instantly responded, "No."

"Hmm, could it be white?" again with the lilting voice.

"Yes."

"Is it squiggly?" Sad voice.

"No."

"Hmmm, is it on the road?" Again, happy voice.

"Yes."

"Is it the lines on the road?" I almost shouted with exuberance.

"Yes!" Berkeley shouted back at me.

"Wow," Kyle said. "Uncle Berkeley, you sure are good at this game."

"He sure is," agreed Rachael.

Worried the kids would eventually figure out my deceptive ways, I gratefully pulled into my brother's driveway as we finished round four. Exhausted, I blew goodbye kisses at them as they ran into the house.

I could tell Kyle still didn't completely understand his uncle, but his compassionate heart wanted to justify his Uncle Berkeley's different ways. I could not ask for

more, and that night I went home with my heart beating
a gentle, even rhythm of contentment.

HELP SECTION

Not reacting to Kyle's frustrations was in one word, hard.
I felt genuinely distraught because he did not understand
his uncle and love him at the same level I did. But
I came to understand that Kyle was not unkind or cruel.
As an exceptionally smart child, he had a strong need to
understand the way everything worked. If things didn't
fit into what seemed normal to him, he felt troubled and
had to resolve the discrepancy in his mind.

As adults we know we should treat those with devel-
opmental delays no differently than we would anyone
else, and sometimes we expect children to automatically
understand this. But their young brains need to question
and reason. Those who have opportunities to help children develop compassion and understanding can greatly
influence how these same children will respond in the
future, not just to your child or loved one but to others
with similar needs.

Be patient. Have talks. Appeal to their compassionate side. Some children need this coaching; others will
take to the interaction very naturally and need very little
intervention. This does not mean that one child is bad
and the other good. A child who does not immediately

understand should not be categorized as those who are outwardly cruel or unkind.

Chapter 20
No Breaks

"We hate for you kids to have to take care of him for a week while we're at the funeral," Mom said.

I switched the phone to my other ear and scrunched my shoulder up to hold it in place while I pulled a pan out of the oven. "Mom, I really think you should go. We can handle taking care of Berkeley for one week. I'll work something out with the other kids."

"I know you can handle it, but it seems like a lot to ask."

"Yeah, but I think you and Dad could use a break. Between the three of us, we can juggle his schedule."

"It would be a lot easier if we could leave him home on this trip," she finally conceded.

"Just go, Mom. We'll figure it out."

I hung up and laid the phone on the counter. In my mind I pictured my parents, young and healthy, taking care of us kids thirty years earlier. Only it had never stopped for them. Their friends went on spontaneous trips; but Mom and Dad, now in their seventies, couldn't even attend an out of state funeral for an aunt without figuring out childcare.

Travel took a lot out of Berkeley and often caused illnesses. Our family vacations had been interrupted many times with stops at emergency departments where only with the aid of intravenous drugs could the doctors get his vomiting under control. Yet my parents had a hard time asking others to watch Berkeley, even their other children, and even for a few hours. They felt he was their responsibility.

A week later I appreciated their commitment even more. Because I lived alone and both Ethan and Leigh had small children, Berkeley naturally spent more time with me than them. However, since I had to be at work during the day, my sisters-in-law welcomed him into their homes. Throughout the week, I fielded several calls as they tried to interpret conversations with Berkeley, understand his bedtime routine and frequent nighttime interruptions, and why he could not eat hot dogs. By the time I got off work on Friday afternoon and completed the hand-off, I almost felt relieved. We had made it to the homestretch and only had two more days to go.

Since Berkeley stayed at my house often, he settled in quickly. But he missed Mom and Dad, and I wanted to make Saturday fun for him.

"Do you want to go golfing, Berkeley?" I asked while I mimicked hitting a golf ball.

"Yeah, maybe restaurant?"

"Sure, Honey," I said. "We'll go golfing and then to Taco Bell, but after that we have to go shopping."

Berkeley disappeared into his room and came out ten minutes later wearing shorts. "Okay, ready to go," he said as he handed me my purse.

In the car I waited for him to buckle in and hit the garage door opener which he enjoyed as much as I had loved hitting the elevator buttons when I was five.

At the family fun center, Berkeley chose a green golf ball, and I let him decide which course we'd play – the winter wonderland or the barnyard option. He chose the winter. Stroke after stroke I could not seem to make anything go in the hole, but Berkeley cheered me on much to the amusement of the couple behind us. "It's okay, Honey," he said patting me on the back. "Maybe next time" or "Ohhhhh MAN!" when I had tried, unsuccessfully, five times to get it through the windmill.

Later as I sat sipping Diet Coke over cheap tacos, Berkeley mimicked my every move. With extreme patience, he waited to sip when I sipped, wiped his mouth when I wiped my mine, and took bites only when I did.

Finally, I played along and asked with fake sternness, "Are you copying me?" His whole body shook with laughter. This joke never grew old. We had played this game hundreds of times.

After lunch, he tagged along while I did my shopping. As we went through the grocery store, he made

suggestions starting with basics like bread and milk.
Then he moved on to hopeful purchases. "Maybe a
donut?" he said with his palms turned up and a shrug
of his shoulders as if this was just an offhand, *Do you
happen to need donuts, Laura?*

I could rarely resist giving Berkeley what he wanted.
So, I feigned ignorance and added a box of powdered sugar
donuts to the cart he pushed. I kept a hand on the back
of the cart always; but even with my precautionary action,
we had a near miss. I looked away every so briefly, and he
almost pushed the cart into the heels of a young mother.

"I'm sorry!" I gasped to her and then turned to
Berkeley, "You have to watch where you're going."

For the next several minutes, he scolded himself over
and over. "Have to be careful. Not do that. Have to be
careful." So intent on correcting himself, he forgot to
pay attention to where he was going; and again I saved
him from running into an elderly man.

Half an hour later, I put the last bag of groceries into
the trunk; and since I had parked directly across from
the cart collection area, I let Berkeley return the cart.

With a crash it settled into place, and Berkeley
turned toward me. When I close my eyes, I can see the
next three seconds play in slow motion — forever burned
into my brain.

Berkeley saw me, and his face lit up as his arms flew
into the air. Like a toddler who momentarily loses sight

of his mother and then spots her, he ran toward me and straight in front of an approaching van.

I felt the scream tear out of some deep place within me. As if I could push him out of harm's way, I thrust my arms forward into empty space and screamed again. I heard the screech of brakes and saw Berkeley jump backwards. For one awful moment, I thought the van had hit him and thrown him into the carts. I covered my mouth to stifle a third scream. For an instant I stood rooted to that square foot of asphalt, my eyes blurred in panic, and then my eyes refocused on Berkeley. He had backed into the carts, and he looked too scared to move. I glanced at the panicked face of the driver who motioned me across, and I ran to Berkeley. My arms wrapped around him, and I hugged him tight — too tightly. I waited until my breath stopped coming in gasps and while Berkeley repeated, "Sorry, Honey. Sorry, Honey."

Then I turned and gave a shaky wave to the driver and mouthed the words, "Thank you. I'm sorry." He drove slowly out of the parking lot.

An older man stood staring at us as I took Berkeley's hand and walked to the car. My whole body shook, and I wondered what this man thought of me. *Does he think I'm careless?*

I had been!

Maybe he isn't judging me. Maybe he was once a caregiver and is sympathetic. It had all happened so fast. My vigilance had only lapsed for an instant, but the feeling of despondency stayed with me for a long time. In a way I previously never realized, I understood in a small way what my parents faced every day of their lives. They could never, ever completely relax. They would be parents until their dying day.

HELP SECTION

Family

You cannot do this all on your own. Find people who can give you occasional breaks. You need to have time to relax — time to go out to dinner or walk on the beach without having to constantly be on the lookout for danger.

Friends/Acquaintances

The parents will probably never ask you to give them a break, and they might even resist an offer at first because they feel such a strong sense of this being "their" responsibility. But they need breaks, particularly if other family members do not reside close enough to give them times of respite.

An important first step involves getting to know the family and the disabled person. This may involve you spending time with the entire family before you offer to take the individual for an outing or even have him/

her over for an afternoon or evening. Imagine yourself as the parent who NEVER gets to stop watching over that person.

Ask as many questions as you like. This will reassure the parents that you understand the magnitude of what you are offering to do. Start out with small outings or short periods of time. This will allow you to build a relationship with the family and the person of special needs. You will gain confidence as you spend more time. Soon, you will look forward to your time together.

Chapter 21
A Phone for Berkeley

"Phone, another job!" Frustration edged Berkeley's voice as he tried to make me understand.

I put my foot onto the seat of the dining room chair and tied my shoe while Berkeley repeated himself for the third time.

"Phone, another job!"

I gave Mom my question mark look, and she interpreted. "He wants a cell phone."

"Oh," I said, looking back at Berkeley, "If you had a phone, you think you could get another job?"

"Yes!" He emphatically nodded his head up and down. "Another job, maybe Lowes."

He already worked four days a week at a job he loved, and we felt afraid that his health might not bear up under a second job, but I tried to put myself in his shoes. Everybody he knew carried a phone, and he wanted to feel like everyone else. He talked about getting a phone a LOT, and he had no qualms of stooping to manipulation. Relentlessly he tried to think of reasons he needed a phone. The "another" job was perhaps his most clever idea playing off our pride in his excellent work ethic.

Shortly before Christmas, I upgraded my phone and added Berkeley to the phone plan. My old texting phone went into a gift bag with Berkeley's name on it, and I hoped he would not be terribly disappointed when he discovered the obvious, that I had pawned an old, used phone off on him.

On Christmas morning, one by one all of us grown-up kids arrived at Mom and Dad's house. As we entered the house Berkeley yelled "Merry Christmas Tree" and then hugged each of us: his brothers, sisters, nieces, and nephew.

He had always been easy to please in the gift department, mostly as happy with new clothes as any kind of a toy we could purchase for him. We loved to retell a story that occurred around his twelfth year. Back then, Amy bought him a six pack of underwear. She disposed of the store packaging and wrapped each pair individually in identical parcels. As he began to open the first pair, she said, "Hey, Berkeley, what ya got there?"

"I don't know," he said with a little bit of awe and wonderment in his voice. He tore the paper off and then, as he held them up for all to see, he shouted, "Underwear," with as much joy as if he had just been told he was going to Disneyland.

As he began to open the second pair, Amy asked him again, "Hey, Berkeley, what ya got there?"

"I don't know," he said. And then the joyful shout of "Underwear" followed.

Six times the scene repeated itself, and by the final pair of underwear, we laughed hysterically at his incredulous, "Underwear!"

Years had passed since the infamous underwear Christmas, and now the house bubbled over with laughing, animated grandchildren. Excitement electrified the room, and Berkeley was not the only one waiting on pins and needles to get at the gifts spilling out from under the tree.

We pulled extra chairs into the living room, and as the gifts disappeared from under the tree, a mound of wrapping paper, ribbons, bows, and discarded boxes filled the middle of the living room. Side conversations and exclamations drowned out any one individual. But we all stopped and looked at Berkeley when he sprang to his feet. In one hand raised above his head, he waved the hand-me-down phone.

"It's a phone! It's A PHONE! My PHONE! Look, a phone. Whooohhh!!!!" For a minute he jogged in place whooping and yelling, and then he rushed around the room hugging everyone. No one person received credit for the phone, but he loved every single person in the room for it and wanted them to share in his good fortune.

Throughout the day, family members took turns calling him. He would fish it out of his pocket, find

the on button and yell into it, "Hello, who's there?"
A 45-year-old brother, in full view of Berk would start
laughing, and Berkeley would exclaim, "Ethan! Why
you calling me?"

That phone went everywhere with Berkeley, and
he talked to everyone about phones. He asked people
he barely knew, "Do you have a phone?" When they
pulled out their fancy smart phones, Berkeley would
say, "I show you," and then reaching into his pocket he
produced his phone. Face beaming, he said, "I have a
phone too."

In vain we tried to tell Berkeley not to talk about
his phone so much, but he couldn't help it, and we
realized that most people enjoyed having Berkeley show
them his phone. Such an innocence and joy about him
made looking at an old worn-out phone somehow enjoy-
able; and usually so limited in communication because
of Berkeley's speech challenges, people suddenly had
something in common, something they could talk about
and share.

As time went on, I began to realize this trait did not
belong to Berkeley alone. I found that those with Down
syndrome generally give off a warmth that is gentle,
calming and somehow, at the same time, joyous.

Several years ago, I sat toward the back of a plane
waiting while the rest of humanity, it seemed, crammed
itself into that metal tube. I sat in an aisle seat and

flipped aimlessly through a magazine when an angry voice demanded, "I need past you!"

Startled, I looked up into the face of a scowling woman. I quickly jumped up to let her squeeze into the row, but unfortunately the woman in the middle seat, absorbed with a game on her iPad, did not hear the exchange.

"Are you going to let me through or are you going to just sit there taking up space?"

Looking incredibly shocked, the woman rose to her feet to let the angry woman through to her seat.

As she plunked down in the window seat, she continued to mutter and complain viciously. The woman next to me started texting a friend about the demon sitting next to her. The tension grew, and people in front of us glanced hesitantly over the backs of their seats. The woman across the aisle caught my eye. I replied with a helpless shrug of my shoulders as if to say, *I don't know what to do.* And then I heard the cabin door click shut.

I felt a twinge of honest panic. The people around me had that same look. We didn't have an escape route, and this crazy lady looked like she might start punching people.

And then, bustling down the aisle came a little man with Down syndrome. As always, I instantly began to draw correlations between him and my Berkeley. He wore a baseball cap. Berkeley rarely appeared in public without his.

"So sorry I'm late. I'm very sorry."

He stopped at the row directly behind me and said, "Oh, excuse me. Excuse me. I in there. Thank you! Thank you very much. So nice. Thank you. Excuse me. Very kind, thank you."

Almost like magic the tension started leaking out of the plane. People looked over their shoulders to get a glimpse of him, and smiles warmed their faces. The uncomfortable hush of seconds before turned into a relaxed atmosphere while everyone strained their necks while trying to eavesdrop on his conversation.

"Can I leave my hat on?" he asked the man sitting next to him.

"Sure, that's fine. We're not in church."

Then, "Do we get a pop to drink?" The man explained that in a little while someone would come by with a cart and let him choose his pop.

"Oh, hmm, Coke. Yes, I'll have a Coke," he muttered to himself, and then as if remembering his manners, he said, "Thank you, very good information. Thank you very much."

The acidic woman in my row also listened. She rose in her seat and turned around.

I held my breath.

"They will give you a choice of peanuts or pretzels too," she told him, her voice softening.

I felt tears springing to my eyes. I had braced myself for the worst flight of my life, and one little man in a baseball hat had unknowingly defused a very toxic situation in the span of about two minutes. I believe if that young man had not been on our flight, there would have been an altercation of some type.

As I sat pondering the events that had unfolded, I wondered how different our world would be if all Down syndrome babies were given a chance to live. Over 90% of these gentle, peace-loving babies suffer the horror of abortion each year. What would our world be like if there were 90% more Downs people in this world of ours reducing the tension of explosive situations. Could it be possible that we would have fewer wars?

During the entire flight, I sat with my head pressed to the back of my seat and listened. This guy's obsession did not revolve around phones but credit cards. He quizzed the man beside him about credit cards for half the trip.

"Do you have a credit card?" Knowing he should not ask, he self-corrected. "Shouldn't ask that, not nice." BUT he could not help himself; so, he asked a follow-up question. "Do you have a Chase card? Very good card, um hmm, Chase card."

I pictured it all so clearly. His siblings and his parents saying, "You can't ask people if they have credit cards. It's not right." So, he knew better, but oh the temptation to talk about credit cards.

He functioned at a much higher level than our Berkeley, but the loving, grateful, pleasing traits existed as strongly as they did with Berkeley. He thanked the stewardess profusely for his Coke and then went on to say, "Very good service. Thank you very much."

When we finally landed, I still questioned whether he had a credit card or not, but I did notice that everyone in our area wore a huge smile.

HELP SECTION
How to Answer Difficult and Inappropriate Questions

1. People often ask, "At what age does Berkeley function?"

    Answering this question takes a lot of thought because Berkeley does not function at any one level. In many ways, he still exhibits childlike behavior and skills. He does not read very well, and we don't turn him loose with matches. We still remind him not to eat too much or he will throw up.

    At the same time, he demonstrates capability in many areas. He does his own laundry, cleans his room, and makes his lunch before heading off to work each day.

    Perhaps we all need to remind ourselves that those with disabilities, much like anyone else, have a strong desire to fit in with others. Guard against treating them as if they are small children. Even though some of Berkeley's behavior remains child-like, he is also an adult and has some of the same aspirations as you and I have: to drive a car, to own a phone, and most importantly, like any human, to be loved.

2. Recently a friend of mine with a disabled grand-daughter told me that a woman in the grocery store pointed at her granddaughter and said, "She is consuming all of my taxpayer dollars." On another occasion, a woman stopped her and said, "No offense, but what value does she even bring?" With tears in her eyes, the grandmother asked me, "What can we say to comments like that?" I thought for a long time about how I would reply, and God gave me three points.

   Point 1: Every human is valued by God.

   - God created your child in His image. God made your child to be like Himself. "So God created man in His own image, in the image of God He created him; male and female He created them." Genesis 1:27 NKJV

   - Not only did God specifically design your child, He expects you, and everybody else, to praise Him for the way He made your child. "For You have formed my inward parts;

You have covered me in my mother's womb. I will praise You, for I am fearfully and wonderfully made; Marvelous are Your works." Psalm 139: 13 – 14 NKJV

Point 2: I ask the person who thinks the world should not include Berkeley to imagine that a car has hit their beautiful, typically developing child. As they stand by the hospital bedside, what kinds of bargains would they be willing to make with God if only He would allow their child to live? Any loving parent would rather take home a disabled child than no child at all.

Point 3: With Berkeley, we can easily point to the way he contributes to society, but what if he could not hold a job, fold his own clothes, and vacuum his own room? Perhaps then he could teach me the greatest lesson of all, the joy in serving another person. When someone cannot give back to you, you learn the valuable lesson of selfless service. Our world is made infinitely better by people who learn to give without expecting something in return.

Chapter 22

Cheerios

Berkeley peered with disappointment into the nearly empty box of Frosted Mini Wheats." Not enough, Honey," he said as he shoved it in front of my nose.

About nine lonely pieces of cereal remained in the once full box. Thinking that a taste of the "Wheats" as he liked to call them would satisfy him, I poured them into a bowl, added some Cheerios, and gave the mixture a stir. Berkeley disappeared into the bathroom; so I set the table for two then sat down at the piano to go over a tricky piece of music I would play later during the morning worship service at church.

After a couple minutes, I gave the keyboard a several measure rest to yell over my shoulder, past the table, and down the hallway, "Hurry, Honey! We don't want to be late for church."

While concentrating on a difficult series of notes, I did not notice Berkeley passing me and heading into the kitchen until I heard a weird rustling coming from that room. Upon investigation, I found Berkeley painstakingly putting each Cheerio back into the box.

"No, Berkeley, you have to eat those. Otherwise, you'll be hungry all morning."

I simply could not take him to church without a proper breakfast.

"Make tummy sick," he replied.

"No, no, Cheerios don't make you sick," and I took the bowl away from him and closed the box." Come on, we have to hurry and eat."

We sat down at the table, and Berkeley reached over and patted my knee. A surge of love for him filled my heart. He was so loving and kind, but a few moments later I scolded him for flicking all the Cheerios off his spoon and back into his bowl." Berkeley, you have to eat those."

With a resigned sigh, he took several bites and then made a run for the bathroom where he gagged until he threw up.

Aghhhh! I did not need this today. When he came back to the table, I said, "That is so naughty, Berkeley!"

In frustration I went back to the piano and played another song. When I turned back to Berkeley, he held his head in his hands and a teardrop rested on his cheek.

I let out a heavy sigh and patted him on the back. I always found it impossible to stay irked with Berkeley. "I love you, Honey," I said as I put my arm around his shoulder.

He instantly pulled the bowl of cereal near and began to shovel the remaining breakfast into his mouth. Between bites he tried to persuade himself that it was okay by saying, "Mmmm, yummy! Yum, yum, good Cheerios." A couple of times he began to gag, but quickly held his finger up in the air and shook his head. He made a strong effort.

While I cleared the table, he brushed his teeth; and we headed for the car. He hit the garage door opener for me, and I backed the car down the driveway. As usual, Berkeley changed out the CD for gospel music. On Sundays Berkeley didn't think he should listen to secular music.

I thought we had won the Cheerios battle, but Berkeley began to remind himself not to throw up. "Naughty to throw up," he repeated a couple of times. He cracked the window for fresh air, and I turned up the heat to balance against the cold air rushing through the window.

We pulled into the parking lot with a few minutes to spare, and I silently praised myself for my good mothering. Putting on my happy church smile, I took Berkeley by the hand, and we entered the foyer. Berkeley let go of me and headed to the men's room while I began to chat with one of the older men.

What followed next felt like a scene out of a movie. The unmistakable sound of retching came from the bathroom. It seemed those Cheerios had found their way to the depths of his being and could not rest until they heaved everything that stood in their way out. No matter how loud or long it took, they were coming out of Berkeley. Valiantly I tried to ignore the sound as if maybe only I could hear it; but with each passing second, the volume of his vomiting increased. I struggled to keep an even flow of words coming while I considered that perhaps instead of possessing good mothering skills, I was instead a cruel, cruel sister who forced her brother to eat himself to an early death. My voice trailed as the older gentlemen I had engaged in conversation looked toward the bathroom and then at me with a puzzled expression. I felt crimson creeping up my neck.

"He isn't actually sick," I said. And then I found myself launching into a long explanation about how Berkeley had once thrown up Cheerios at the start of a nasty flu bug, the events of the morning, and the frustration associated with the way his brain still functions like a child's even though he had already turned 31 years old.

Berkeley had tried so hard to keep his breakfast down. I knew he had tried, but all his self-lecturing and flagellation had only made him think about it more and more until in the end the only thing he could think about was throwing up Cheerios.

Over the next few months, as soon as Berkeley arrived at my house, he quietly made his way to the pantry. I would hear the door creak open and then the shuffling and opening of boxes. Each week Berkeley checked to make sure I had an appropriate cereal waiting for him. But just in case, he also packed a small bag of breakfast cereal for himself.

HELP SECTION

Parents

A Down syndrome child functions well with boundaries and rules, but an area of his brain does not function like a typical child's brain. You must learn to differentiate between situations like the Cheerios scenario and actual defiance. Sometimes, you may fail at making the correct distinction; but all parents fail from time to time. Be sure to extend some grace to yourself! Berkeley did not hate me after the Cheerios episode.

For Berkeley, a short circuit seemed to exist in his brain when it came to certain foods. All he could remember was that one time, this or that made him throw up. Additionally, certain foods such as pancakes stuck in his throat due to the artificial portion of his esophagus. Later when we had to have his esophagus stretched, the doctor informed us that he found food lodged in his esophagus. As he described it, we were horrified to realize he had eaten that food for dinner the previous day.

Friends/Acquaintances

Please, please extend grace to your friends and do not chock up every behavioral misstep to poor parenting. Bear in mind that not only mental but physical disabilities contribute to the child's behavior.

Also remember the unfathomable patience you must exhibit with toddlers. Many parents of a disabled child have already hit their golden years, and their child never grew out of the toddler stage. For 10, 20, 30 or even 40 years, they have continued to parent the child they love so much who never grew up. And sometimes, yes sometimes they are tired — bone weary of being patient.

Chapter 23

Esophagus

The whole Cheerios incident got the family talking about Berkeley's esophagus, and we decided maybe we should set up a doctor's appointment. Given the surgeries he had undergone as an infant, we could never hope it would work properly; but it did seem like things had taken a turn for the worse.

With a sigh, Mom made an appointment. And who could blame her for that sigh? Berkeley had so many doctor's appointments — appointments for his psoriasis, asthma, hearing, eyes, scoliosis, recurring boils, and disks slipping in his hips — the list seemed unending.

After his initial stay in the hospital as a baby, Berkeley had relatively good health; but he had many smaller chronic problems that left my parents feeling as though the doctor's office had become their second home.

Mom scheduled the appointment. And a few weeks later, Berkeley went through a series of tests including an endoscopy of his esophagus and a barium swallow test.

While Berkeley was still groggy from medication, the doctor pulled a chair close to Mom and sat down. "His esophagus is very abnormal." He laid a hand on Mom's wrist and continued. "While we examined his esophagus, I took samples for a biopsy. I am concerned the cells may be cancerous."

As Mom repeated the conversation to me on the phone later that night, I tried not to panic. I worked with doctors, and I knew the devastation of esophageal cancer and that very few people at that time recovered from it. Berkeley's risk factors made him more susceptible to the disease, and I did not want to even imagine our Berkeley having to go through treatments.

Throughout that long weekend, while we waited for the test results, I cried desperate, incoherent prayers to God begging Him to let the tests be negative.

On Saturday, as usual, I picked Berkeley up from my parents and brought him home with me. At bedtime, I sat on the edge of his bed and read a story from the Bible to him.

How much did he understand? I was never sure, but I wanted him to know God. Through the years I had done my best to introduce him to God. Often, I asked him if he knew who Jesus was and what Jesus had done for him.

"Jesus is God's Son, Berkeley, and He died on the cross for us. He died because we have all done bad things, and only He can pay for our naughtiness."

I showed Berkeley pictures of the crucifixion, the empty tomb, and depictions of Jesus leaving the earth.

"Jesus is making a place for us to live when we die. It will be very beautiful, and everyone who knows God will be there."

"Grandpa and Grandmom with Jesus?" he asked.

"Yes, Berkeley. Grandpa and Grandma are with Jesus because they loved Him and asked him to take away their sins."

Then we quoted John 3:16 together. *For God so loved the world,* "That means everybody, even Berkeley and Laura," *that He gave His only begotten Son,* "that's Jesus" *that whosoever* "that's you and me Berkeley," *believeth in Him should not perish,* "perish is a fancy word for die" *but have everlasting life.*

That evening, Berkeley pointed to a picture of Jesus in the book. "Grandpa and Grandmom with Jesus?"

"Yes," I said, "Grandpa and Grandmom are with Jesus."

Then he pointed to himself and said, "Berky and Jesus."

Berkeley had never told me that he would be with Jesus. He had never made the connection to himself.

On any other day I would have been elated; but that night, fear squeezed my heart. A bitter taste came into my mouth, and my pulse began to pound in my eardrums. Had God just sent me a sign? Was God telling me that Berkeley would die but not to worry because he would be with Jesus.

God, I cried in my head, *please not that. Please don't take Berkeley away from us.*

I did not tell anyone what Berkeley told me, but I agonized over his words — alternately taking comfort from his recognition of what God had done for him and fear that I would lose him. Christian friends assured me of their prayers for the outcome of those tests, but the waiting wore me out.

When Mom called me at work Monday afternoon to let me know that his esophagus, although problematic, was free of cancer, I broke down and cried.

A co-worker saw my tears and fear flashed across her face. She whispered her one-word question, "Berkeley?"

"He's fine," I said wiping my nose and smiling. "I just heard he's fine. I don't know why I'm crying; I'm just so thankful."

Word spread quickly throughout my office, and the people who loved the stories I told about Berkeley came by to tell me how happy and relieved they also felt.

I knew that if the results had shown cancer, our family would band together and face it like we did with his other challenges. This time we didn't need to.

HELP SECTION

Friends/Acquaintances

In times of trial and fear, please do not give reassurances to the family that are not yours to give. During some of our scariest periods of time, people have told us that everything would be okay. But they had no way of knowing the outcome or having power to make things alright. Letting the family know that you care and pray for them comes across as more authentic than empty promises you cannot keep.

Chapter 24

Laura Moves

The legs of my chair made an unnaturally loud scraping sound against the tile as I scooted back from Mom and Dad's dining room table. Without saying a word, I went to Berkeley's room and sat on the edge of his bed gazing at him while he watched television. *Why did life have to be full of such hard choices?*

My employer had been asking me to move to the East coast for years. This time the request turned into less of a request and more of a requirement — my job would probably disappear if I didn't make the move.

They knew, however, that I played an important role in Berkeley's life and that this decision ripped at my core. In the most gracious way possible, they did everything in their power to make the move manageable in my unusual circumstances and even offered to fly me back and forth every two weeks for a few months. At the end of the trial period, I must decide whether I would move for the job. If I did, I would be under a binding contract that would keep me on the other side of the country for two years.

I discussed the relocation with my family many, many times over the course of those months, and unanimously they encouraged me to make the move.

"You need to live your own life, Laura. This is your chance, and Berkeley is our responsibility, not yours." Dad did not want me to throw away my career because I felt responsible for Berkeley.

"We'll really hate to see you go, Laura, but Dad is right," Mom said.

Part of me wanted this adventure, wanted to live somewhere else and see what could happen. At the same time, I could not shake the feeling that perhaps selfishness drove my decision. I wanted to see where life could take me if I didn't consider Berkeley. I had always known that if something happened to my parents, I would never abandon him; but I also wondered if this contributed to my singleness. Although it was unlikely that Berkeley would outlive my parents, my siblings and I had agreed long ago that I would take on his care when and if my parents became unable to do so.

A little piece of me always wondered if the possibility freaked men out. To be fair, I did not blame them. I tried to imagine taking on the responsibility of somebody else's disabled child, some pretend person I did not know and understand. What would it be like to have this person in my home, always making plans around them and taking care of them?

If I, already knowing and loving Berkeley, struggled with wondering how I would adapt to someone else's disabled child, I could understand why this would be a huge thing for a man to consider. I had grown up with Berkeley and loved him all his life. If I were to marry and then have Berkeley live with us, he would not be "our" child together. I understood this would be a tremendous ask of anyone, and only a kind, compassionate, loving person would willingly take on such responsibility.

Berkeley looked at me and interrupted my train of thought, "Pay Day Friday! Want to eat at a restaurant? Want to do that?"

Unshed tears flooded my eyes. *Yes, Berkeley! Yes, I do want to celebrate every pay day Friday with you. You are not a burden to me. No sacrifice I've ever made has been too much, but I'm moving away. I won't be able to eat out with you anymore.*

I knew then my decision had been made. Several weeks later, my parents came to my little yellow house and sat with me while strangers showed up to purchase household items. I saw Berkeley's eyes widen in shock as strangers carried his bed out the front door, and a piece of me wanted to run after those outsiders and scream for them to put it back. Tears filled my eyes as I remembered how Berkeley used to take the pink bedspread off as soon as he arrived and stow it in the closet. He refused to sleep under a pink blanket, and I finally replaced it with a green comforter.

The memories hit me hard. All the breakfasts we shared together – how he mimicked my every motion and bite until I said, "Hey! Are you copying me?" And each time he laughed at the old joke.

Every part of leaving him behind tore me up; and as if the internal pressure didn't wreak enough havoc, friends and acquaintances began to question me. "What about Berkeley? Won't he miss you?" One man told my parents he did not understand how I could abandon Berkeley.

This man could not know how I had lain awake at night dissecting my decision again and again. Could he know how I struggled with guilt and misgivings?

Early on an August morning, I fought the deep ache in my chest as I stood over Berkeley's bed. Wondering for the thousandth time if I would ever live close to him again, I stooped to kiss his cheek. He stirred and reached an arm around my neck and kissed me goodbye. He had been sound asleep, and we had said "goodbye" the night before; but I could not leave that morning without saying it one more time. Already I missed him in a despairing way.

On the way to the airport, I sat silently in the passenger seat and let the tears drip into my lap. Deep down, I knew Berkeley would adjust; he always did. He would develop new routines that did not include spending the night at my house on Saturday night, and those routines would make him happy.

Our new normal became talking on the phone for a few minutes every three or four days. The conversations were predictably similar. I listened while the phone rang five or six times. I pictured him fumbling around to turn off his television, unplug his phone from the wall, and wipe the saliva from his lips with the back of his hand before pressing the talk button. A slight pause and then he yelled for my parents' benefit, "I've got it!"

"Hello, Honey! Hi, Honey! Lowa is that you?"

"Yes, Berkeley, it's me."

"Hi, Honey! How are you?"

"I'm great, Berkeley. How are you?"

"That's good, that's good. How are you?"

He always asked me how I was at least twice, and I pictured him making his way across the room to his calendar. My coming home for the Fourth of July and Christmas would happen without doubt, but every other holiday or special occasion needed negotiation. So, he tried for everything – his birthday where he would tell me how old he would be, Halloween where he tried to throw in the possibility of a party, and Thanksgiving which he always followed with his ridiculous impression of a turkey "gobble, gobble" and a giggle while he waited expectantly for my answer.

"No Berkeley, but I'll come home for Christmas."

"Okay," he'd say, "That's okay, Honey. Time flies."

Months later, Mom told people, "Well I'm pretty sure Laura misses Berkeley more than he misses her. He does talk about her a lot, but he has adjusted. He always does." A little bit of me wanted him to miss me as much as I missed him, but mostly I was glad he did not feel as sad as I did.

HELP SECTION
Parents/Family

This is a hard subject, but resentment can occur when all the focus and every decision revolve around your disabled family member.

After two years and for a variety of reasons, I made the decision to return to the Northwest, but I will never regret the time I spent away. Those years showed us how resilient Berkeley is. If even harder life changes come his way, he will, in his typical unselfish way acclimate to whatever life throws at him.

Asking Berkeley to fit into our lives and schedules helped make our lives normal while bringing up a disabled child. Of course, we did make exceptions because of his unique needs, but we did not cater everything to his liking. In the end, this made him more adaptable and flexible.

If your child has many special needs, you will find it important to find ways to recharge your own battery. Most states in the United States provide some respite care by trained professionals. Taking advantage of these benefits is not a shirking of your responsibility.

Friends/Acquaintances

If you are not part of the inner circle of decision makers, please keep your opinions to yourself. You have no idea the amount of guilt and pressure a family may be under during some of these life-changing decisions. You cannot know all the intricate details that go into the simplest decisions. Unless abuse or neglect is occurring, please do not inflict guilt on a family that has to make difficult decisions.

Chapter 25
Not Too Dangerous

After nearly 20 years of Berkeley working at a sheltered workshop recycling cardboard, the facility lost its land lease and could not afford to move and set up at a new location. Berkeley had a few months to make a transition before the establishment completely closed its doors; and Mom, Dad, and I had many lengthy talks about what kind of work Berkeley could do.

In a few months, I would move back to the Northwest, but I took a week of vacation anyway from my job in Tennessee and spent it with my parents and Berkeley.

"I guess we need to find you a new job," I said to Berkeley.

"Mmh," he answered unintelligibly but clearly with distress.

Berkeley loved work — he loved the entire process starting with diligently making his lunch each evening for the next day. Sometimes he cleared the dinner table before others finished eating so he could pack up favorite leftovers and put them into his insulated lunch box.

Other times he constructed cheese sandwiches with lots of pickles and mustard. To complete his lunch, he added a can of soda and then looked in his birthday cupboard.

Ethan at a loss for what to buy for Berkeley one year, since he already had every piece of sports equipment and more clothes than he needed, had landed on the idea of buying him lunch treats. Soon the rest of us siblings copied Ethan's idea, and Berkeley had a huge store of individually packaged cookies, cakes, and chips.

"Dad, cash?" Berkeley asked.

"What do you need cash for?"

"Come on, Dad! Cash for bus," and Berkeley held the palm of his hand upward toward Dad and wiggled his fingers. His left hand rested on his hip and an expectant smirk crossed his face. This was all a part of the almost religious ritual that took place each evening after Berkeley finished making his lunch. Dad fished a dollar bill out of his pants pocket, and Berkeley carefully tucked it into his Velcro wallet which he placed on the edge of his dresser.

"Thank you!" he said in exaggerated exasperation.

The next morning as the bus rolled into the driveway, Mom shouted, "Berkeley, your bus is here."

Berkeley, in his room watching TV, stood to his feet, turned the television to Channel 3, and then turned it off. According to Berkeley, the TV must be on Channel 3 when in off mode. He slipped into his jacket, donned a baseball cap, and slid his wallet into his pocket. He walked straight to the kitchen and retrieved his lunch and then kissed Mom and Dad goodbye.

If you took time to walk to the picture window, you would see him stoop down to pet the cat before he crossed the lawn to greet his bus driver. Even though the bus was a special one and picked Berkeley up in the driveway, Berkeley had an amazing sense of independence as he went through the normal routine of going to work.

On one of my vacation days, I volunteered to pick Berkeley up early for a dental appointment. As I pulled into the parking lot, I saw him in his orange vest, surrounded by a mountain of cardboard. I sat for a minute and watched him throw the stacks of it onto a conveyer belt. He kept at his work in a steady, measured pace.

On my way into the office, I waved at Berkeley; but he stayed focused on his work and either ignored or didn't see me. I introduced myself to his supervisor, Ann, who told me how hard Berkeley worked.

"At lunch time he helps some of the other workers heat up their lunches and get settled; but let me tell you, he's always the first one back to work."

I smiled while she told me this. Everything about what she said was consistent with Berkeley. He liked to be helpful and above all he loved a schedule.

Ann stood up from her desk and walked outside to call Berkeley.

Berkeley paused and looked my way and then started aggressively waving his arms in an away motion. "Not 3:30," he yelled at me. "Take bus home."

"No, Berkeley," I called back and now waved my arms in a 'come here motion.' "We need to go see the dentist about your teeth. We have to leave now."

Head hanging low, as if the world had done him wrong, Berkeley resignedly walked toward the office.

I had come a few minutes early allowing him time to take off his vest and hang it neatly on a coat hook, retrieve his lunch box, and make the rounds to tell everyone goodbye. As I watched his comfort level at work and his carefully established routine, I wondered how we would ever find another job so perfect for Berkeley?

In the coming weeks we talked to Berkeley often about finding a new job. Usually, Berkeley adapted better to change if we gave him plenty of notice, and already he had been matched with a job coach who searched for jobs Berkeley could not only do but would enjoy.

Berkeley had his own idea about jobs he wanted to do. For years he had asked us if he could get a second job working at a hardware store. He primarily wanted it because he thought everyone who worked at hardware stores needed a cell phone. We now chased after this dream, but it didn't work out.

One evening I sat on the couch brainstorming with him about possible jobs, and he came up with a new idea.

"Cop," he told me.

"You want to be a cop?" I asked with obvious skepticism in my voice.

"Too dangerous?" he asked, his head tilting to one side.

"Yes, Berkeley. Yes, being a cop is very dangerous."

He sighed and disappeared into his room.

I didn't think it would come up again; but the day before I flew back East, I wandered into the kitchen to talk to Mom. While we stood chatting, Berkeley popped out of his room. He held something behind his back, and I craned my neck to see what he hid. He didn't leave me in suspense long.

"Cop with Andy," he said as he held up a DVD of the Andy Griffith Show. "Cop with Andy, NOT too dangerous."

As he took his DVD back to his room, Mom and I burst out laughing. "You have to admit, he would make a pretty good Barney Fife," I said.

"Just so long as he doesn't carry a gun and leaves that one bullet in his pocket like Barney did," Mom replied.

Berkeley didn't get his job fighting crime, but he landed another dream position in a large business café. He bussed tables, filled napkin holders, and put away the clean pots and pans. He quickly learned to love his new routine, co-workers, and clients. His new supervisors often commented on his excellent work ethic and praised the good work he did.

Since the café gave Berkeley free lunch, he didn't need to make a lunch; but other than that, his routine stayed pretty much the same. He still asked Dad for cash each evening, and Dad pretended he didn't know why. He would put the cash in his wallet; and in the morning, when his bus arrived, he turned the TV to Channel 3 and then off, told Mom and Dad goodbye, petted the cat, and greeted his bus driver.

HELP SECTION

Although you may think the activities of a person with a disability appear cute, please refrain from using that terminology. Higher functioning people with Down syndrome find it demeaning; and while many of the things that Berkeley did could be called cute, he never liked to be called cute. When people tell him, "You're cute," he emphatically replies, "Not cute. Not a baby."

Chapter 26

Berkeley Lost

As I pulled out of the church parking lot, my phone began to ring. Fumbling through my purse, I located the wireless blue tooth just as the phone went silent. I pulled to the side of the road before sticking it in my ear and hitting the call back button.

As I merged back into traffic, Mom's familiar voice came across the line.

"Hey Mom, I'm just coming home from a late choir practice. Did you need something?"

"Not really" – a long pause — "We kind of had a crisis tonight. Everything's okay now. We almost called you, but we knew you couldn't do anything. You would have just gone out of your mind." She talked fast and in short, disjointed sentences.

"Wait, Mom. What are you talking about? What happened?"

"I'm sorry. I'm just rattled. Berkeley went missing for several hours tonight."

For months Mom and Dad had struggled with the government run bus system, Access. The Access bus, supposed to pick Berkeley up from his job each evening, sometimes showed up as much as two hours after Berkeley finished his shift. But he had to wait and watch alertly until it arrived. Making things even more difficult for Berkeley, they often sent a cab or a different kind of pickup service. With the constantly changing vehicles, Berkeley became used to getting onto a variety of vehicles.

"It got so late and still Berkeley didn't get home," Mom said. "So, I finally called and asked the dispatcher to tell me how much longer until we could expect him home, but the dispatcher didn't know. Access started making phone calls and discovered they had never even picked Berkeley up from work. I called his work, but they had closed and didn't answer the phone. Access dispatched a supervisor to his workplace to check on him, but they couldn't even get inside the dark building. They conducted a city-wide search of all their transportation vehicles, but none of their vehicles had Berkeley."

Even though Mom had already assured me everything had turned out okay, I felt my pulse quickening and my body begin to tremble. I found a parking lot and pulled under a gigantic Magnolia. Barely aware of the cicadas humming in the background and the intense Tennessee heat, I gripped the steering wheel and with clenched teeth listened while Mom finished the story.

"We called Berkeley's phone over and over, but it just kept going to his voice mail. Finally, Access called us back and told us they had contacted the police to file a missing person's report. They wanted me to describe what he wore to work, and they asked for a recent photo."

My insides went cold. I had imagined this nightmare but never believed it would happen. Every worst-case scenario ran through my head.

"We were frantic, Laura! We wanted to call you," she repeated, "but we knew there was nothing you could do, and you'd just go out of your mind."

I tried to imagine what I would have done. Seattle — in all its vastness — where would one even start to look? I imagined him being abused, and I could hardly breathe. How do people live through something like that?

"Finally, my phone rang again," Mom told me, "and a woman on the other end said, 'I am with a young man here who is struggling with his phone. It looks like you have called him many times.'"

As Mom told me that part of the story, tears sprang uncalled to my eyes. Mom continued by telling me that the woman — that angel — said she would stay with Berkeley until my parents could get to him. We could never know for sure everything that took place. But apparently, he waited a long time. When the bus didn't come, he decided to try to get home by getting onto a Microsoft shuttle. He toured from Microsoft campus to Microsoft campus. Knowing he was not in the right place, he got off one bus and showed his Microsoft badge to get onto another bus. His phone, somehow turned to silent, did not ring. As his anxiety mounted, he forgot how to make phone calls. At last, this woman noticed him desperately trying to make a call and stepped in to help him.

"We drove like crazy people," Mom said. "We drove really fast and ran lights; and when we got out of the car, he couldn't stop hugging us. It was awful! We got home just before I called you."

When tears from my eyes dripped onto my hands, I repeated to myself, *He's safe! He's safe!* But I could not stop crying. I felt as if I had lived through it, those horrific anxious hours. My body began to physically react. Waves of nausea flooded over me, and I opened the car door and leaned over the pavement. *He's safe; he's safe,* I told myself again. *Thank you, God, for keeping our Berkeley safe.* But still, I could not stop crying.

HELP SECTION

Over the next weeks, our family took many measures to make sure we would never face that place of fear again. We bought Berkeley a new phone which he could more easily navigate and which had a tracking system on it. We got him signed up to ride in a van pool with amazing people who took a personal interest in him. Yet we knew there was still so much that could go wrong. But we had to let him live his life. The reality remains. Berkeley will NEVER grow up, but we cannot keep him in a bubble.

Parents

Every day you will face decisions. Some of the decisions you make will be great, but sometimes you will feel you have failed. You get to decide how much independence to allow. What is too risky? What if you decide wrong? Know that you won't get it right every single time. Nobody does! Not even if your children are typically developing. Allow yourself some grace to make mistakes.

Friends/Acquaintances

Remember to pray for the moms and dads whose babies never really grow up. My parents would not trade Berkeley for anything or anybody, and as a family we've always seen Berkeley as a special gift from God. He has made our lives better in so many ways, but there are hard days. Please be slow to judge and quick to offer your support.

Chapter 27

Berkeley's Sandwich — September 2016

Life with its many twists and turns brought me back to the Northwest. After having lived independently for more than 20 years, I moved temporarily into my parents' home and set up an office on the upstairs landing. At 5:00 each morning, I stumbled out to the hallway and logged onto my computer to take the first phone call of the day. With effort, I could almost make my voice sound like I'd already been up for as long as my East Coast colleagues who had undoubtedly dressed, showered, and had presumably drunk a cup of coffee. In the quiet of the early morning, I powered through spreadsheets and reports until 7:00 a.m. when, in the bedroom below, I heard Berkeley's rooster alarm sound — my signal to noiselessly run down the carpeted stairs, grab a yogurt and coffee from the kitchen, and cart it all upstairs without Berkeley detecting me. I had to act unsuspecting, so Berkeley could "sneak" up the stairs behind me.

"Good morning, Honey!" I felt his arms hug my shoulders.

Turning in the chair, I raised my hands in feigned surprise. "Good morning, Berkeley! How did you sleep?"

"Good, good!" He planted a kiss on the top of my head and then retreated downstairs to take up his own morning routine. Welcoming me to the day had introduced a new element into his schedule.

After a bowl of cereal, Berkeley brushed his teeth and dressed in his uniform. With sounds cluing my imagination, I saw him switch on the television and settle into his easy chair. Soon, I heard the "I Love Lucy" show blasting from his bedroom. He never grew tired of Lucy and Ethel's impossible schemes, and I loved hearing his laughter because in his words, "They are so funny!"

Shortly before his ride arrived each day, he spent several more minutes in the bathroom combing his hair to perfection before cramming a hat onto his head. Many times we stood on the other side of that door yelling for him to hurry; but the hair, all part of the routine, had to be combed just so.

I heard the rattle of his bus crossing our bridge.

"Berkeley! Your bus is here." Mom yelled. "Hurry!"

Berkeley grabbed his wallet and came to the bottom of the stairs. "Goodbye, Honey!"

"Goodbye, Berkeley! Have a great day. I love you!"

Mom and Dad received goodbye kisses too. Then he left for the day, and the house became strangely quiet. I looked forward to his return.

As I sat at the top of those stairs, I tried to remember when my parents had last taken a trip by themselves. I could easily get Berkeley off to work and be there for him when he arrived home each day. After 49 years of parenting (including all of us older kids) they deserved some time away without children. And so, upon my insistence, Mom and Dad took advantage of my presence to take a well-deserved vacation.

The week flowed along smoothly until Thursday at lunch time. Berkeley had Thursdays off, and at precisely 12:00 noon, he climbed the stairs to my "office" and said, "What's for lunch, Honey?"

I glanced at my watch. Lunchtime already? I needed to finish a project and didn't have time to stop and make him lunch.

"Oh Berkeley, I'm really, really busy right now. Do you think you could make yourself a sandwich?"

His forehead furrowed while he thought it over, and then he answered. "Yes, Honey! Yes!"

"Oh, that's great, Sweetie. I'm really busy."

As he turned to leave, my stomach growled. I half turned and grabbed his hand. "Do you think you could make a sandwich for Laura too? Maybe a cheese sandwich?"

This took more thinking because everything processes slowly for him.

Then he smiled, "Sure, Honey."

"With pickles?"

"Sure, sure, Honey! Be right back." He patted me on the shoulder and clumped down the stairs. Below I heard sounds of cupboards opening and closing, the door to the basement creaking, a jar scraping across the counter, and finally his feet padding up the stairs behind me. In one hand he carried a plate with a cheese sandwich cut perfectly in half. A small pile of crackers sat beside the sandwich. In his other hand he carried a glass of water.

"For you, Honey," and he laid a napkin on my lap.

Later that night I lay in bed trying to fall asleep while listening to the drone of Berkeley's television set. He did not live on East Coast time and had a couple of hours until bedtime. I could not decipher what he watched, but occasionally I heard the mellow sound of his laughter, and the simplicity of his world spilled into mine causing peace to rest in my heart.

A few minutes earlier, he had come up to tell me goodnight. I supposed the rest of the world would think it odd, him knocking gently on my door and then coming in to kiss my forehead. But his kindness and caring personality were not odd. Thinking about the beauty of his person filled me with contentment.

I tried to imagine a world without Berkeley and his counterparts with Down syndrome. The very thought made me restless and suddenly uncomfortable. I turned on my side as if the physical readjustment could bring back my peaceful state of mind. I lay there and thought about the lunch he had prepared for me, his big sister. All his special touches spoke to his gentle caring nature: his trip to the basement for a jar of pickles, the way he cut the sandwich in half, and the crackers and water to complete the simple meal. Because I always use a napkin, he had found one of those too and brought it to me.

Berkeley's mind will never solve complex problems. He struggles with change, and routines provide a safety net for him. But Berkeley cares for people in an astounding way. If Mom, or Amy, or I had a new dress, Berkeley never failed to say, "Wow! New dress." He always noticed before anyone else.

Caring for Berkeley does require additional work. Some people have pointed this out as if that sums up his existence. And while there is some truth in the fact that my parents will grow old worrying about his health and making sacrifices for him, something balances out those cares and tips the scale the other direction. Why has Berkeley's lunch stuck in my head? Because it represents the thousands of ways he touches our lives with his love and his joy in serving others.

"Did you have a good time?" I asked my parents when they returned from a week at the Coast.

"We did, but...."

"But you missed Berkeley?"

"We really appreciated you watching him, but vacation didn't seem like vacation without Berkeley."

HELP SECTION

Parents

Encourage self-sufficiency in your child, and they will surprise you with how much they can do on their own. Even though it may take extra long to accomplish things, they will walk away with a sense of pride; and with practice they will become faster and more efficient. Additionally, you have also laid foundational stones for their future job or even independent living. Nurturing moms may struggle with this the most, but you will do your child a big favor if you let them learn to butter their own bread, cut their own meat, make their own bed, etc.

As your child begins to speak, work hard not to finish sentences for them. I've found that Berkeley appreciates answering questions. If the person he's talking to doesn't understand, then he looks to me as an interpreter.

Friends/Acquaintances

Be patient and allow for mistakes. Imagine how you would feel if every time you wanted to learn a new skill, someone told you, "You don't know how to do this, you'd better just let me do it." Or if every time you fumbled with your keys, someone took them away and said, "Here let me do that for you." As you exhibit patience with your friends with disabilities, their confidence will grow.

Chapter 28

Van Pool Crisis

"Laura, can you call the van pool and let them know I'm going to be late to pick Berkeley up?" I could hear the stress in Dad's voice as he blurted out that the main road had a tree across it, and a lengthy detour would slow him down.

I glanced at my watch and then looked for a safe place to pull to the side of the road. Since I had made the arrangements for Berkeley to ride in the van pool and because my parents didn't have texting phones, I acted as a liaison and relayed messages between my parents and the van pool.

Five minutes before Berkeley should arrive at the meet-up point didn't give me much time. I shot a text message to the van pool coordinator and nervously stared at my phone waiting for a response that did not come. I tried calling, but my call went to voice mail.

I had a phone number for the driver, but knowing he probably wouldn't answer while driving, I pulled out my back-up plan and called Berkeley.

Anxiously biting the bottom of my lip, I listened to the phone ring — once, twice, three times, and finally mid-fourth ring, I heard static and the background noise of a vehicle and lots of voices. I waited for the cheery, "Hello, Wowa!"

"Hi Berkeley!"

"Oh, hi, Honey, how are you?"

"I'm fine. Can I talk to Ken?"

"No, Tim not coming today."

"Oh, okay, Berkeley, can I talk to somebody else on the van?"

"Okay, bye, Honey."

"No, Berkeley," I shouted, "don't hang up!"

"I'm fine," he responded. Clearly, he had removed his hearing aid when he answered the phone.

"Berkeley, I need to talk to somebody else in the car!"

"Okay, bye, Honey."

"NO, NO, don't hang up! Berkeley, give the phone to somebody else."

I gripped the phone and pleaded with him to hand his phone to anybody in the van.

"Okay, here, Kevin."

At last I heard a male voice say, "Hello."

"Hi, this is Laura, Berkeley's sister." I rushed on forgetting Kevin would not likely hang up on me. "My Dad is on his way to meet you, but the road is closed. He's having to make a big detour. When you drop

Berkeley off, could someone walk him into the gas station and tell him to wait there for my dad?"

"Sure, no problem."

Whew! Or sort of whew. I called Dad again to let him know the plan, but then I began to worry and pray. I hated these variables. Would Berkeley really understand that he needed to wait, and what if he had to wait a long time?

My phone rang again, and this time I heard Ken, the coordinator, on the other end.

"Hey, Laura. Sorry, I have the day off. What do you need?"

"I think it's under control," I told him. "I spoke to somebody. Berkeley said, it was Kevin."

Ken's dry chuckle broke apart a bit of my pent-up anxiety. "Yeah, that's the other Ken, Driver Ken. For some reason Berkeley calls me Tim and him Kevin, but we just go with it."

"Oh brother!" I felt my brighter version of a chuckle matching his. "That does clear things up a bit. I assumed you must be the one Berkeley calls Tim. I've tried to correct him, but he seems emphatic that your name is Tim and that the driver is Kevin. Berkeley talks about you both but always refers to you as Tim and Kevin. Now that I have the code, I'll know who he means."

"Ah, he's a good kid. We like him a lot. He's quiet most of the time except that every day he points out a big pile of wood we pass. Every day he wants all of us to notice it."

"That's so Berkeley," and I allowed myself to laugh again even though anxiety still gnawed at my insides. "Berkeley loves to split wood. He's probably trying to tell you he's been splitting wood for the neighbor. When he and I take a walk together, he shows me all the tall trees and wants somebody to cut them down with a chain saw so he can split them."

"Oh, and to think I just thought he really liked wood."

This time we laughed together and said our goodbyes. As I threw the phone onto the seat beside me and pulled back into traffic, I continued to pray Berkeley would make it home safely.

A few minutes later, driver Ken texted to let me know they had also been stuck in traffic so arrived at the meeting point just when Dad arrived.

God had answered my prayer and again kept Berkeley safe.

HELP SECTION

Parents

Start constructing the biggest/strongest safety network you can possibly build. Get your child comfortable with friends and extended family. In a crisis, they will be more adaptable if they have already spent time with these people.

Friends/Acquaintances

Do you live close enough to pick up the child/adult from school or work should something happen? If you have the capacity, let the parents know you are willing to be a resource in a transportation crisis.

Chapter 29

Berkeley Sick

"He started throwing up as soon as he got home from work last night."

"Diarrhea?"

"At first," Mom answered. "There's nothing left in him now. Mostly he just vomits gastric fluids."

I returned Mom's grim look and then walked to the back of the house and quietly opened Berkeley's bedroom door. His restless hands twisted the bed sheets pushing them up and down. He turned his glassy eyes toward me but did not greet me. He half sat up, retched into a bowl, and then fell back onto the pillows. He did not ask me to empty it — just turned his head away.

"Oh, Honey," I said, as I instinctively reached my hand to feel his forehead and smooth his hair. The room reeked, and I found myself holding my breath.

"It's okay, it's okay. I'm fine," the sound came out in a hoarse croak, and I could see his body already suffered from dehydration.

I took the bowl and rinsed it in the bathroom. Within ten minutes, he would need it again.

"How long are we going to let him vomit?" I questioned my parents. In my head, I calculated the time. If he started the prior evening, he would have been at this for over 12 hours.

"I hate to call now," Mom said. "They'll just tell me the flu is going around and to wait 24 hours."

"We already know it's not going to stop. We need to take him in now and get him started on IVs. Have you ever thrown up for 12 hours straight?" Frustrated at the anger in my voice, I immediately felt guilty. I knew better than to direct anger at my parents — my exhausted parents who, well into their 70s, had spent another sleepless night worrying and taking turns stripping his bed, rinsing the bowl, and trying to ease his pain.

None of us felt like sitting in an urgent care clinic on a weekend. How many times had we done this while Berkeley sat miserably slumped in a vinyl chair vomiting into a garbage can?

In the early days, we waited the 24-hours as instructed by the on-call nurse. Unfortunately, this only extended Berkeley's agony — once vomiting for three days straight and almost costing him his life.

"I'll go with you," I promised, "but we leave now!"

"I hate for you to give up your one day off," Mom said; but I could see the relief in her eyes.

Dad started toward Berkeley's room to change him into clean pajamas. Knowing we would be gone for a minimum of eight hours but probably longer, Mom packed protein snacks and water bottles.

"Dad, I think you should stay home and rest up. Somebody will have to look after him when we bring him home."

"I hate to make you and Mom go by yourselves."

"Nah, Dad, it won't do any good to have all three of us there with him. Stay home. Rest. We'll call you."

As I drove, I kept one eye on Mom and Berkeley in the back seat and mentally prepped myself for the first crucial moments at the triage desk. In a mixture of politeness and firmness, we had to convince the staff that we were not just another overprotective family who ran to the doctor every time our child coughed. We needed the nurse to understand that Berkeley could not stop vomiting without medical intervention, no matter how long we waited.

Berkeley, often relegated to the back of the line with all the minor colds and sniffles, had many times sat in misery as the hours slowly ticked by. However, if I could make them understand his history, the doctors could get ahead of the severe dehydration by giving him IVs of anti-nausea medication and fluids to rehydrate his dangerously ill body. This could mean the prevention of a hospital stay.

Nearly four hours later, the triage nurse popped out of her office, looked at Berkeley and said, "What are you guys sitting out here for?" She walked over to another desk, and I could see her gesturing at us while she spoke animatedly to the staff. Berkeley's body convulsed as he retched into the garbage can I held.

I wiped his mouth and waited for the nurse to walk back to us. "I'm so sorry you've had to wait. You will see a doctor very soon now."

Whatever she said kicked people into action, and in a short time another nurse ushered us into a private room where a doctor arrived a few minutes later. Trying not to sound like an overprotective sister, I started reciting Berkeley's current symptoms and his long history of medical issues.

Berkeley, now too weak to sit, started retching. I pulled him upright so he wouldn't choke. The doctor murmured his sympathy, and immediately ordered the hydrating fluids and anti-nausea medication Berkeley needed.

For the next five hours, the clinical staff monitored him closely. Each time the anti-nausea medication wore off, he began vomiting until at last he didn't. Determining his body was appropriately hydrated and that he had passed the danger zone, they sent us home. Mom and I eased him back into the car praying that we had gotten him through the worst of this flu and could avoid a hospital stay.

I buckled Berkeley in before climbing into the driver's seat. Glancing at Mom in the rearview mirror, I could

tell that every part of her aching body cried out for rest.
Nobody in their 70s should still have to sit up with sick
kids; but weary as she was, I watched her reach over
and smooth the blanket on Berkeley's lap.

After helping settle Berkeley into bed, I left with a
weary and worried heart. I knew my parents had come
close to their limit of endurance, and I wondered when it
would become too much. They so rarely asked for help;
and if I had not popped in for a visit, they likely would
have taken him in on their own. I feared the extra stress
would cause them to become sick too.

Each day that week I called for an update, and
thankfully, Berkeley did not relapse. The following
Saturday, when I pulled into the driveway, I saw Berkeley
shooting baskets at the end of the garage. When I shut
off the car, he came to the window and kissed me on
the cheek.

"Can I work on Monday?" he asked.

HELP SECTION
Parents

Know your limits. Especially as you age, you will not
always be able to be everywhere and do everything. If
you have other children, let them take a turn sitting with
your child who has a disability. Accept the meal someone
cooks for you or the offer to mow your lawn.

Friends/Acquaintances

A few ideas of how you can be helpful during an illness.
Drop by the hospital with a sandwich and some prepackaged snacks and drinks, offer to watch a pet that may need attention, or stop by their house and mow the lawn.
Once everyone comes home from the hospital, stop by their house with a meal, mow the lawn again, and take the dog for another walk. Hospital stays exhaust the parents. They'll appreciate these gestures, and you'll provide tangible support.

Chapter 30

The Joy of Christmas

"**M**aybe Saturday, 10?"

I placed the last few pieces of pepperoni onto our evening meal and shoved the pizza into the oven before looking at Berkeley.

"Maybe Saturday, 10, shopping?" he asked again.

Wiping my hands down the length of my apron, I looked at the calendar Berkeley held in front of me.

In large, uneven letters he had managed to write "Shop" onto the 10th of December. "S-H-O" ran across the top, and then he squeezed the "P" in crookedly underneath. But he had managed to fit the entire word into the square allotted for the day.

"Sure, we can go shopping next Saturday."

"Oh, yeah, yeah! Good, that's good," he replied. "And um, maybe a sandwich, chips, pop, cookie and a pickle?"

Even though lunch was an established part of the tradition, he felt compelled to confirm it. We had done this for so many years that I already knew what he would order: a ham and cheese sandwich, chips (never the apple), pop, and a cookie shaped like a mitten (they only serve the mitten cookies at Christmas time).

Because of his methodical ways, I also knew the exact order in which he would consume his lunch — first the pickle. Then he would remove all the vegetables from his sandwich and eat them separately. After finishing his sandwich and chips, he would break off the thumb of the mitten and give it to me. When finished munching (me long before him since I only got the thumb), he would look at me and say, "Okay, let's go."

On Saturday morning of December 10 – a date set in stone since it had been inked onto his calendar, I drove to my parents' house. A light flurry of snowflakes dotted my windshield. *How perfect!* I told myself.

Just as I expected, Berkeley had dressed in his typical "go shopping" clothes (his green plaid shirt and blue jeans) and waited for my arrival in anticipation of our fun, Christmassy day.

At the sandwich shop, Berkeley stepped up to the counter with confidence, and the young gal behind the cash register smiled at him and then me.

"Are you Christmas shopping today?" she asked.

"Yes, Wowa!" He said pointing at me.

"I'm his sister, Laura. We always come to Panera when we go Christmas shopping. It's our tradition, isn't it Berkeley?" I nudged him on the shoulder, and he nodded in affirmation.

I explained to the girl that I had some rewards points I wanted to use. "I earned them at another store. Is it okay if we use them here?"

"Absolutely," she assured me and then listened intently while Berkeley ordered, looking to me often for interpretation. When she tried to apply the rewards points, however, something went wrong. Even the manager could not get them to record and after a couple of minutes she said, "Don't worry about it; I'll just write this off."

"No, no!" I argued, "I'm happy to pay. I can use them another time." But they waved me aside and smiled at Berkeley. This happened all the time; no one could resist his charm.

When the young worker brought the sandwiches to our table, Berkeley thanked her; but I instantly noticed a missing element – no pickle!

Since everyone had shown such kindness, I didn't want to bother them again. Quickly I decided not to say anything unless Berkeley mentioned it.

He didn't seem to notice, and instead pulled the veggies out of his sandwich and ate them before biting into the bread and meat. Predictably, after finishing his chips, he broke the thumb off the mitten and handed it to me.

As we left the store, two or three of the workers smiled and waved.

I tapped Berkeley on the shoulder and pointed to them. He paused in the open doorway; and as a gust of wind blew past us, he turned, smiled, waved with his palm wide open, and hollered, "Merry Christmas tree!"

A few hours later we had purchased presents for his nieces and nephew, Mom, Dad, and his sister-in-law, Loretta. Berkeley had insisted on buying Loretta a bag of M&Ms. She had always been his favorite, but I suspected he didn't want her to steal from the "Ms" he always received on Christmas day — like she had the year before.

At my house, Berkeley settled his things into his room, plugged his phone into a charger, and then set to work wrapping the gifts. His stubby fingers struggled with the scissors and tape. But when he finished, he proudly set them under the tree.

Together we stood admiring his handiwork, and then he brushed his hands together in satisfaction of a job well done. "Call Mom?" he asked.

"Sure, you can call Mom."

Even a phone call follows a well-orchestrated process. Carefully Berkeley removes his hearing aids and stashes them in his pocket. Then he unplugs his phone and swipes through screens until he finds Mom's picture. With a staccato tap, he hits her photo. He watches. It is not dialing; so, he tries again. On the third try, he hits it with the correct amount of pressure, and the phone dials. He puts the phone to his ear and holds an index finger up in the air while he waits for her to answer.

"Hi Mom! I'm sorry, no pickles. They were ALL out of pickles. I'm sorry, no pickles."

I wonder what Mom thinks. She has heard out of context statements from him for a lot of years, and she probably figured it out. She knows his routines and what disturbs him. I hear indistinct words coming through the receiver. Berkeley repeats himself. "I'm sorry. No pickles." I hear more of Mom's voice before Berkeley tells her, "I love you, Mom. Take care, Mom. Bye."

Well, I guess he had noticed that missing pickle!

Two days before Christmas, I bought a few last-minute groceries and ended up walking down the condiment aisle. Knowing everyone in my family would think I was the absolute worst gift giver, I bought a big jar of dill pickles. I put them in a gift bag with Berkeley's name on it and hauled it out to Mom and Dad's house.

On Christmas Day, I pulled gifts from under the tree and helped Berkeley distribute the ones he had bought and wrapped. I continued to pass out the remaining gifts while Mom and Dad's living room echoed with laughter, oohs, and awes. Tissue paper, ribbon and bows abandoned their former glory and lay crumpled on the floor. We were winding down — content and ready to spend a relaxed day.

Somehow Berkeley's usual pile of videos, M&Ms, and socks did not interest us as much as our many side conversations until Berkeley startled us by jumping out of his chair. "Look!" he shouted. Conversations halted, and we stared at him holding the jar of pickles above his head for all to see, "It's pickles!"

We laughed and cheered with him and then reminisced about the time he got six pairs of underwear and the time he got his "new" phone. Once again, he brought his unique spark of joy to the holiday; and from then on, he would always have a jar of pickles under the Christmas tree.

HELP SECTION

Friends/Acquaintances

One of the most encouraging things you can do for a family is to accept and include their loved one who has a disability. But try to take it a step further by treating them as equals. Ask them occasionally what or where they would like to eat. Allow them to sit in the front passenger seat. As they become adults in biological years, make a place for them at the grown-up's table. This shows how much you value them as a person and will speak volumes to the family about your ability to see beyond a disability.

Chapter 31

Berkeley's Movie Moment – Saying Goodbye for Now

When sentimental movies play, an image sticks in my mind. I picture a grown son standing in the driveway. Behind him the parked car sits packed and ready to go, but the son does not move. My throat tightens as I prepare to witness the defining moment. The young man has changed from a boy to a man. He wants to say so much to his parents, but words seem elusive.

His eyes meet with his dad's, and then he, the son, sticks out his hand. His father's hand tightens over his in a handshake.

Everything that happened in the movie flashes through my mind, the struggles, the happiness, and now the goodbye. The son wants to tell his dad what he means to him. He wants to say, "Thank you, Dad, for being there when I was sick, for helping me with my homework, for coming to my ballgames, for loving me when I was a jerk, and for loving me when I wasn't a jerk. Thank you for all you've done for me, for the sacrifices, and the unconditional love." But those words escape him; so instead he utters three simple words, "Thank you, Dad." And the dad understands that they mean, "I love you."

Berkeley adores sappy movies. I think he loves them because they celebrate life's special occasions, and he especially loves movies that contain big life events — new babies, weddings, and funerals. Often, he calls us to his room to watch those special "movie moments" with him.

He comes out to the hallway and says, "Honey, come here, I show you." I sigh, but rarely do I deny him the pleasure of sharing because this is one of his ways of communicating. In his bedroom I perch on the edge of his bed and watch the tear-jerking event.

He also plagues my parents with, "Mom, Dad, you have a minute?" They, like me, trek into his room and with amazing patience watch the same scenes they have already seen a hundred times.

Recently, my parents cleared a patch of land. Dad revved up the old tractor and tuned up the chain saw. Berkeley climbed aboard the tractor and rode to the far end of the pasture with Mom driving. She let Berkeley off, and he stood a good distance back with Dad and cheered for her as she pushed trees around with the tractor. Then for several hours, Berkeley helped pull branches out of the way after Dad limbed them with the chain saw. Berkeley enjoys physical labor and working with his parents more than any other activity.

That evening while Mom finished up the dishes, Berkeley made his way out to the garage where he found Dad puttering around. When Dad noticed Berkeley standing there, he said, "What do you need, Good Guy?"

Although Berkeley has not always had the ability to verbalize his feelings in words, somehow, he usually managed to let us know them anyway.

That day Berkeley stepped forward and held out his hand, small and tough. For a brief second, Dad looked at him puzzled. Then he extended his own hand, enormous and rough; and it eclipsed Berkeley's in a handshake. He and Dad stared into each other's eyes. And then Berkeley said, "Thank you, Dad. Thank you very much."

In many ways, Berkeley would always remain a little boy, but another part of him had grown into a man, a man who would leave a print of love on the heart of every person he touched.

The End – But Not Really

Although we are saying goodbye to you for now, Berkeley continues to write the next chapters of his life by living a happy and full life. His life, his effervescent spirit, his routines, his love, and his gentle nature permeate our lives as well. We are blessed to call him ours.

HELP SECTION

Parents

Don't stare too hard into the future. Don't project yourself 20, 30, or 40 years from now and try to imagine what life will look like. You may not realize yet what a great gift you've been given, but you will. And when you do, you will look back at your younger, doubtful self and wish that you could go back and tell that person to relax and enjoy the moments as they came because those moments - they turned out great.

Made in the USA
Middletown, DE
22 August 2024

59012877R00128